733

FROM HEGEL TO TERRORISM

FROM HEGEL TO TERRORISM

And Other Essays on the
Dynamic Nature of
Philosophy

by
James K. Feibleman
Tulane University

HUMANITIES PRESS INC.
Atlantic Highlands, N.J.

First published in 1985 in the United States of America by Humanities
Press Inc., Atlantic Highlands, NJ 07716

©Copyright 1985 by Humanities Press Inc.

LIBRARY OF CONGRESS CATALOGING IN PUBLICATION DATA
Feibleman, James Kern, 1904–
        From Hegel to terrorism and other essays on the dynamic nature
of philosophy.

        Includes bibliographical references.
        1. Philosophy — Addresses, essays, lectures. I. Title.
B945.F23F76   1984   100   83-26655
ISBN 0-391-03056-4

MANUFACTURED IN THE UNITED STATES OF AMERICA

For Stanley C. Feldman

TABLE OF CONTENTS

FOREWORD

CHAPTER

FOREWORD

Philosophy as we know it today has taken itself out of the main-stream. It has given up all theoretical consideration of practical affairs and left that important task to the Marxists, who use it as an instrument of propaganda and justification. Their official version does not allow for any other philosophy in the countries they dominate. At the same time, in Europe and America there has continued to be a classical tradition of realism. Begun by Plato and Aristotle, it was reinforced by the method and the findings of the physical sciences. More recently it was recognized by C.S. Peirce and organized by A.N. Whitehead. Unfortunately, it has fallen out of fashion: philosophers have preferred to concentrate on the linguistic or the psychological aspect of things.

No one thinker can correct that situation, but a start can be made. To explain what philosophy, even of the most abstract variety, has to do with the price of eggs has been my aim in many published volumes and remains my aim in this one. Metaphysics, for example, one of the class of master theories, meets practice only through the mediation of some special theory, such as economics, politics, aesthetics, or theology. That is why it has been thought to have no application.

I wanted to show the power philosophy exercises over events, even in extreme cases. Society is the result of so many separate developments that its course cannot easily be predicted, but it does interact with philosophies, and it can be charted by them. I have chosen the topics in this volume deliberately at random in order to illustrate my thesis.

There is, of course, more to it than that. In his *Aspects of Prehistory* (Berkeley, CA, 1974), Grahame Clark wrote, "In modern societies the fragmentation of knowledge has to some extent been overcome by philosophical systems." It has not; but it should have been. In some 18 separated but related volumes, I have tried to supply the lack.

Chapter II was first published in *Tulane Studies in Philosophy*, vol. XXX (1981). Chapter III was an invited address to the Charles S. Peirce Society meeting in Boston in December 1980. Chapter V first appeared in *The Philosophical Journal* (Glasgow), 13, 117-124 (1976). Chapter IX first appeared as an essay in *Perspectives in Biology and Medicine*, vol. IX, 537-548 (1966).

CHAPTER 1

RECENT FASHIONS IN PHILOSOPHY

The position of elder statesman, or, as it is called in academia, emeritus, carries with it the privilege of personal access to a generous portion of recent history, and hence to a long-range perspective on fashions in philosophies as these have come and gone. The general effect is depressing. Seniority affords ample protection against taking any one philosophy too seriously, for what is prominent today may very likely be forgotten tomorrow; but there is the additional fact that philosophy itself is no longer recognized outside the profession. A newcomer ignorant of all this is apt to take the most recent revelation as a final word. And so it is — for awhile; though as it turns out, he who commits himself to the total acceptance of a currently fashionable doctrine is likely to end in disillusionment. To save him I would ask him to look briefly with me at the historical list of philosophical preferences as they have succeeded one another during the last century.

Seven philosophies in turn have dominated that period. The seven are: neo-Hegelian British idealism; neo-Kantianism and the epistemology of C.I. Lewis; Kierkegaard and existentialism; logical positivism; phenomenology; pragmatism, and Wittgenstein and the philosophy of ordinary language. Each of these in its day had prevailed over the social and intellectual scene. There is some overlap, but the period of dominance runs about twenty years — roughly a generation. Each one assumed that its favorite thesis was paramount, that no other point of view was necessary or need be expressed, and that appointments in the universities were to be made accordingly. I will have occasion to mention several other philosophies which have received lesser attention and hope to show the reasons why that was the case; but first, these seven. I mean to describe the aspect of reality which brought each into prominence and what occasioned its downfall, and then to follow this discussion with some general conclusions. These cameo sketches, however, are intended only as reminders and not as full representations of the philosophies named.

I

At the turn of the century, Hegelian idealism as set forth in the writings of F.H. Bradley and Bernard Bosanquet dominated the English-speaking world. I take it that the type case was the publication in 1893 of Bradley's *Appearance and Reality*. For Bradley, reality was distinct from appearance, without contradiction, and made up of a whole which is more than the sum of its parts. Bosanquet agreed that there is a systematic rational totality to all experience, in which all natures find their explanation. The two levels of feeling and thought were resolved in the third level of the higher synthesis of the Absolute.

The merit of British idealism was that it called attention to the organization of thought. We do think in terms of wholes, and we do try to see the elements disclosed by experience as parts. Life and reason together demand a system of ideas which is both consistent and comprehensive. Only philosophy can provide it, and does so best by means of an idealistic philosophy.

The demerit was that organized thought is by no means all there is; the material world also exists with all of its vividity, conflict, and force, and was neglected altogether. The reality of contradiction was denied, but contradiction is real, if for no other reason than because it has real effects. One might well come to the conclusion from a study of the British idealists that life is a neat package with all of its edges smoothed out and that the findings of philosophy have nothing to do with the market place.

II

Before Kant, British empiricism and continental rationalism had belonged to separate traditions. Kant endeavored to put them together in subjective terms. He tried to go beyond experience to explain experience, but he did so in terms of self-conscious knowledge. For Kant there is no direct experience of the world. Time, space, and the categories interpose themselves between the observer and what is observed, conditioning experience by laying down the elements by means of which it can take place. The result is that we can never know the world as it really is, but only as it appears to us. Beyond all the phenomena there are noumena which must remain forever unknowable.

C.I. Lewis in *Mind and The World Order* (1929) sought to relieve the unmitigated solipsism of Kant by recourse to practicality. The categories by means of which we experience the world are pragmatic; they were made by the mind, and they can be changed by the mind. We interpret our experiences as social products.

The merit of Lewis' view is that it preserved what there was of value in Kant. We do hold our philosophies subjectively, and this remains true whether the philosophy itself is subjective or objective. The mind is where we consciously recognize what we believe and where we harbor the thoughts from which we intend to act.

The demerit was the retention of the closed subjective circle for all thought, one that still left the flavor of solipsism and failed to account for anything that lay outside the accepted scheme of things, including surprises and the unfamiliar. As in idealism, to which it is related, the material world with its conflicts and forces remained unexplained.

III

Kierkegaard was dead by 1855, but the effect of his existential philosophy was felt only much later. For him, only the individual is real because only the individual exists. Feelings of anguish and a sense of alienation are the evidences of the individual's primary reality. Against the rational works of the philosophers, the individual in his solitariness must accept responsibility for his own decisions. The consequent estrangement, anxiety, and despair are marks of his reality and can be met only by an act of faith: the individual, as such, is the very meaning of existence.

The merit of existentialism is that it restored to the individual his rightful place. He *does* have an authentic ontological existence which had been overlooked in the swirl of social, economic, and political philosophies: he *does* count and he *is* real.

The demerit is that this view was too narrow and did not include a fitting of the individual into the proper social and cultural setting. The similarity of existentialism and mental illness has been noted, though the identification is with the patient rather than the physician. It can explain neither the world nor man's place in it.

IV

In the 1920s there was a group of philosophers in Vienna called the "Vienna Circle." Led by Moritz Schlick, Rudolf Carnap, and Otto Neurath, they were responsible for advancing a philosophy known as logical positivism. Building on the positivism inherited from Auguste Comte, that scientific knowledge was the only genuine knowledge, they insisted that philosophy must confine itself to a doctrine of meaning resting on empirical verifiability. They thought in terms of a logically perfect language and took as their model the language employed in the science of physics. Whatever had no empirical reference was, quite literally, non-sense. Hence traditional metaphysics was dismissed, as were many other topics in philosophy.

The merit of logical positivism was that it recognized the importance of the kind of knowledge discovered by the scientific laboratory method of observation and experiment. Science at the center does provide an ideal, even though at the edges scientific knowledge often remains vague and indefinite.

The demerit was that it sought to limit all knowledge to this one kind, as though all moral effort, artistic impulse, and religious spirit had nothing of truth to offer.

V

Phenomenology as a comprehensive philosophy was ushered in by Edmund Husserl (1859-1938) and extended by his student, Martin Heidegger. For Husserl, the key concept was the intentional consciousness. The mind differs from physical objects in being a set of tentacles attached to objects: consciousness is a matter of meaning, and Husserl withdrew meaning into the inner consciousness. The ultimate experiences are the intentions of the subjective ego, but philosophy recognizes that its products are common characteristics, not individual things. Heidegger's further reduction of 'being' to 'human being' left nothing more to be investigated in the external world.

The merit of phenomenology is that it reminds us of the intimate connection between consciousness and meaning: that consciousness has its own meaning, even if the value of this insight is to warn us that there is a perspective involved in knowledge which must be accounted for.

The demerit was that it limited philosophy to conscious meaning. There is a wide world out there independent of our knowledge of it, and we had better recognize its overwhelming importance. Heidegger reinforced the strong German tradition of subjectivity and gave it a new authority, thus diminishing the claims for attention of other schools.

VI

Pragmatism has been the only native development in American philosophy. The idea was contributed by C.S. Peirce, who also invented the name, but the philosophy itself was popularized by his friend and disciple, William James. For Peirce, pragmatism was a theory of practice; if a proposition is true, he thought, it can be applied successfully, and the way to determine its truth was spelled out by physical scientists in the laboratory. William James, who had a more practical turn of mind and was much more interested in getting things done, read the principle differently: what works is true, he said. But converting the proposition in this way altered its import completely, for a theory has to be discovered from experience before it can be practiced. The most useful procedures in medicine were not discovered by the bedside physician but by biologists: antibiotics, tranquillizers, penicillin. The discovery of nuclear energy was made by theoretical physicists, not by engineers.

The merit of Peirce's pragmatism is that it connects theory with practice, seeking to utilize the scientific method in philosophy for its tentative rather than its absolute conclusions. Thus the version offered by Peirce was the correct one: theory does precede practice.

The demerit of James' version was that it made truth dependent upon practicality, an outcome of which we can never be certain; for a truth may seem to work for awhile and then suddenly fail, as in fact happened with Mussolini's fascism.

VII

The last and most currently fashionable of our seven twentieth century philosophies is that of Ludwig Wittgenstein and the philosophy of ordinary language. Wittgenstein's *Tractatus* (1922) was an effort to show how propositions are derived from facts. It has not proved as influential as his second book, the *Philosophical Investigations* (1953), which is an analysis of the meaning of language. Gottlieb Frege had earlier described the two functions of language: meaning and reference. Of these, only meaning had been emphasized by this school, even though reference was the topic of the earlier *Tractatus.*

The merit of Wittgenstein's work is that it called attention to a much neglected area: the nature of meaning. Fortunately for the efforts of the analytical philosophers, generally the study of the meaning of language has linked up with the engineering enterprises of information theory and of telecommunications.

The demerit is that it de-emphasized the role of reference, even though reference is as important as meaning and in the opinion of some may be even more important. For language arose as a way of dealing with the material world, and it continues to be used in that way.

VIII

I should say something here about the two other philosophies, realism and Marxism, which are, in a sense, special cases because neither has ever been dominant in western Europe or America.

Realism rests on the theory that there are two equally real ontological strata: the universe of individual material things and forces interacting in space and time, and a second domain of completely abstract logical and mathematical objects, such as universals and qualities, all of which are seemingly independent of both space and time. Our knowledge of this second domain was derived from our experience with the first universe. The scientific method of investigation has served as a technique for learning about the abstract laws by means of which we control concrete facts.

Two realists have been prominent in developing this philosophy, C.S. Peirce and A.N. Whitehead. There have been German members of this school of thought also, men like Alexius Meinong and Nicolai Hartmann, but they were overshadowed by the prevailing German preference for subjective philosophies.

The second special case of important philosophies is by long odds the most prominent. Since the nineteenth century, Marxism, so far as Europe and America were concerned, has lain offshore but was officially adopted in many Asian countries, notably in the Soviet Union and China, beginning in 1919. That it has flourished in Asia was due to its political sponsors: it never caught on in either Europe or America, where it has been considered to lie outside the area of legitimate interest because its acceptance was due more to force than to reason. The tendency of philosophers in the west, therefore, was either to accept Marxism, which is rare, or to neglect it altogether, which is more common. This last attitude may be a mistake, since on technical grounds it can be refuted but because of its political support will not go away.

IX

Fashions in philosophy have in common advantages as well as disadvantages, and I mean to comment on both, leaving a final judgment to others.

First, then, the advantages. Every new philosophy has something fresh and hitherto unrecognized to say about the nature of things. From a fresh perspective, neglected truths emerge, and they make legitimate demands on attention. For it is true that a culture never recovers its equilibrium after the shock of a great philosophy. Things now are seen differently, and values rearranged. The advent of a new philosophy always means that there has been some progress, for it invariably brings with it new insights which are worth having and preserving. The problem is always how to evaluate the new arrival and fit it into the existing body of knowledge.

And now the disadvantages. In order to promulgate a new truth, the claims of a philosophy must somehow be exaggerated; in order to be recognized as an insight, a philosophy must insist on being the only one. Every fresh philosophy must perforce be overstated, a neglected pebble chosen to be the chief cornerstone. What has a legitimate place must claim, in order to gain attention, that it occupies the only place, for that is the way movements in thought work.

The limitations of all philosophies, then, is their insistency on absoluteness. The claim to the absolute truth has been effective in politics and religion, but it has been fatal in philosophy. Not only do philosophies represent the truth, but also the whole of truth. The assumption of truth is an old tradition in European philosophy, so old that it hardly needs stating explicitly, for it is always assumed. A philosophy is its own proof; that it exists, and has adherents who do not doubt it, is assumed to be evidence enough.

By implication, if not openly stated, the denials of a philosophy are always wider than its claims. There shall be no other philosophy before me, each seems to say. All overlook the fact that the world is larger and contains more than has ever been encompassed in a single system, however comprehensive. By not abating its claims and allowing for the possibility of progress in the discovery of truths, each philosophy dooms itself to failure with the emergency of the very next member of the species.

Philosophers are, by the very nature of their profession, competitive where they ought to be cooperative. Philosophy ought to advance as the physical sciences do: by drawing larger and larger circles to include all previously discovered knowledge as special cases, rather than by repudiating all previous claims.

Currently, the errors in procedure are to be found in two places: in university appointments and in peer review. The first error consists in the use of jobs as a weapon, handing out appointments in philosophy departments as a reward for agreement. At one time in the not too distant past, Oxford University was said to have had some seventy-five philosophers, all persuaded of the primacy of ordinary language. Surely an ideal department of philosophy would have as many diverse advocates of known positions as there are diverse philosophies.

The second error in precedure is the choice of a criterion for the making of decisions by referees of papers submitted to professional journals, which are usually based on agreement rather than on competence. The criterion of agreement guarantees a monotony of product, and operates as an obstacle in the way of all originality. That may be the reason why the pages of most journals of philosophy are so dull, and why the articles they contain are counted toward increases in pay and promotions in rank, but are not read. Why read them when it is possible to predict so accurately what they will say?

The impact made by the astonishing successes of the physical sciences has acted as a watershed in philosophy. Some, like the logical positivists, have come down on the side of the sciences, while others have rejected it altogether. With certain rare exceptions, notably Whitehead and Popper, the philosophers who have concerned themselves with science have thought it their duty to explain to the scientists what the scientific findings mean, but they have not looked at the old metaphysical categories, such as matter, mind, and universals, to see how these could be helped by the scientific findings. Instead, they have sought out ways of doing philosophy which leave the old metaphysical concerns far behind.

The chief lesson to be learned from this brief survey of fashions in philosophy is that, however attractive the current favorite, it will not be one for very long, at most not more than a generation. This fact of history would lend credence to the working principle that Peirce advanced and Whitehead seems to have believed, the principle of fallibilism: whatever a philosophy asserts should be as tentatively held as it is in the physical sciences.

Supporting evidence comes from a survey of religions; those currently accepted in one culture or another should be enough to convince the most sceptical that the claims to the absolute truth, far from being rare, are actually the cheapest things in the world. Therefore, philosophers ought to regard it as their primary obligation to call attention to the danger of accepting any philosophy as final. In a period of rapid social change, such as our own, this ought to be obvious.

Philosophies and cultures interact; philosophies are in a sense expressions of cultures and in their turn affect them. Hegel's philosophy was interpreted by the British as a kind of self-sustained idealism: it put them to sleep because it did not seem to call for any action on their part. That same philosophy was interpreted by the Germans as a call for violent action, and so they made a revolution, first in Russia, and later elsewhere. Both philosophies, as well as both societies, have been profoundly altered by the exchange in ways with which we are now familiar.

Cultures and civilizations are moved by philosophies, but only at deep levels and through long periods of time. The educated and cultivated citizens of western Europe and the Americas pursue their lives in accordance with the prevailing customs and institutions of the societies in which they live and in relative independence of current fashions in philosophy. It is a fact that none of the seven philosophies I have mentioned here have been founding philosophies, that is to say, none have seriously and permanently affected the beliefs and actions of most of the individuals in the societies in which they arose and flourished. Marxism, by way of contrast, surely has; and though many outside the communist bloc of nations have considered it shot through with errors and disastrous effects, none have seen fit to fight fire with fire, to oppose dialectical materialism with a later version of materialism which might better explain and defend the values currently cherished in the western world.

In all the fashionable philosophies we can see one principle at work: all tend to be *true in what they affirm and false in what they deny*. Their truths may be more limited than they had supposed, but they are truths nonetheless; yet the insights are not preserved, and progress in philosophy, as a consequence, is not a cumulative enterprise. All of the previous merits are abandoned with each new point of view that comes into vogue. I am not suggesting that a synoptic philosophy can be didactically collected: it must have more organization than that; but I am suggesting that philosophy could be an open-ended inquiry and a hypothetical proposal. The accomplished philosophical thinker must not only be familiar with the history of philosophy; he must also use it.

CHAPTER II

AN ANALYSIS OF BELIEF

In this chapter I will try to show the range and the reach of beliefs, which I will argue always involve the whole individual. Organs are only the agents of organisms. The individual acts through his parts: he thinks by means of his brain, he feels through his senses, he acts by means of his muscles. Yet on every occasion, no matter which part is leading, the entire man is always engaged. Nevertheless, it should be possible to classify and discuss (I) the various ways in which beliefs are acquired by means of thought, feeling, and action; (II) how they are held in the memory as retention schemata; and (III) how they issue in individual behavior. In a final section (IV), I will look briefly at the social aspects of belief.

I

Beliefs are acquired by means of (a) thought, (b) feeling, and (c) action.

(a) Beliefs are acquired by means of thought.

To be led through a deductive argument is to reach a conclusion which it would be difficult not to accept, always provided one had earlier accepted the premises. This is a conscious, active, and even deliberate process, and it can lead to many kinds of belief. Also, of course, the beliefs accepted in this way can then be combined with others which had been already accepted, and so a thickly woven matrix of beliefs can result. A system of philosophy, such as Kant's or Hegel's, comes to be believed in this way.

There is another way in which beliefs can be acquired through thought. This is the method that employs inductive inference. A better name for it is insight, a sudden illumination resulting in the belief in a novelty. The startling self-revelation of a connection between items already known and accepted is an unconscious process, and generations of original thinkers and discoverers have reported personal experiences of this sort. It usually happens to individuals already steeped in the existing knowledge of a field when they are presented with problems arising at the frontier. In this way new knowledge comes into existence and becomes part of the body of belief.

The most important mental operation regarding belief is called decision. Thought is a kind of voluntary decision-making. Decision operates between learning occasions to select propositions for consideration, and again between memory occasions to determine which propositions shall be adopted by belief. The firmest beliefs, those which can boast of the most rational and factual grounds for their acceptance, are those which lead the most easily to action, but feelings, too, are often involuntarily.

Peirce made the point that beliefs are involuntary. One is not free to accept them or not; the decision to do so is made in terms of reason. In opposition to the contention of his friend, William James, particularly in James' book *The Will to Believe*, Peirce maintained that there is nothing voluntary about belief, which can be accepted only for what appear to be good reasons. This need not mean that they *are* good reasons, only that they *appear so* to the believer.

The fact that what people want to believe they often succeed in accepting is evidenced by the long and successful history of astrology. It has, like many falsehoods, a romantic appeal, and so has gained many followers. Salesmen are notorious for being able to "talk themselves into" the superior worth of what they are selling. This is particularly true of the best salesmen. If one who is working for Buick happens to be fired by the firm which employed him, and is lucky enough to cross the street and get himself employed by Oldsmobile, it will not take him long to convince himself that the Oldsmobile is a better car than the Buick, for only so can he hope to succeed in convincing his customers. Nevertheless, this takes place at a superficial and self-conscious level and does not cut very deep.

False beliefs do gain acceptance for awhile, though most of them are short-lived. The good citizens of Salem, Massachusetts in the seventeenth century, who testified that they personally witnessed witches riding across the town on broomsticks, did believe that they saw what they said they saw, but the tradition did not stand for very long.

(b) Beliefs are acquired by means of feeling.

We are close here to the generic character of belief, which I have already defined as the feeling that a proposition is true. It does not occur in such didactic terms of course, but is more like what we have come to call a conviction. This is the active acceptance by feeling: we know when we are convinced of the truth of something, that the something could be either a reason or a fact, the validity of a reason or the recognition of a fact. We often feel it is right. Thus it can happen that a belief is simply a prejudice adopted emotionally and afterwards defended by means of logical fallacies. The prejudice is reinforced by the tendency to accept as true whatever is asserted, a tendency which can be accounted for quite easily by the fact that every proposition tacitly asserts its own truth.

There is also the phenomenon of passive acceptance. When a slow feeling creeps up on an individual in such a way that he is convinced of a truth without having anticipated it, a truth which comes disguised as a value, he has arrived at a belief. Truth is the logical correlate of value, value the qualitative correlate of truth. The 'proposition' we have been talking about can occur as a qualitative acceptance, in which its nature as a logical proposal is concealed. The best example here might be the audience for the performance of a long musical composition, a quartet, or a symphony, or it might be the reader of a long, cumulative novel. The order of belief in the case of a work of art has this character, for while it can never be reduced to logical or factual terms, it does have a content which is recognized and accepted by the feelings.

Degrees of belief are subject to measurement, for beliefs range all the way from the most casually and briefly entertained suspicions to the more desperate convictions for which one is prepared to die. Extreme beliefs such as the latter are accepted only by means of extreme procedures. There is a psychic shock involved in a religious conversion, and it usually occurs only under conditions involving extreme emotional stress.

Beliefs arise at every integrative level in virtue of the sheer existence of the organism. The neurophysiological concomitants of belief range from the faintest memory traces to those integrations which occur at the highest levels of the central nervous system. The physical belief in the steady support offered by the earth arises from the very nature and function of the musculature. A visceral belief in the prospect of obtaining food makes itself evident in hunger pangs. And finally, the acquisition of language rests on an implicit belief that other individuals who share it also exist.

(c) Beliefs are acquired by means of activity.

These can be passively or actively obtained. Life is action, and there is not much the individual does or could do that does not carry a degree of conviction. If one does not think a bridge will hold, the test is to walk across it. Almost everything the individual does, every activity in which he is deliberately engaged, will convince him of a truth and henceforth demand from him a degree of belief.

Passively, we are all the helpless subjects of actions which lie partly or wholly beyond our control. Natural occurrences, gentle or violent, must carry their degree of conviction, as they impose their effects on the individual who happens to be in their way. It would be difficult, indeed, to believe that a dinner or a hurricane that one had sensually encountered did not exist.

The inception of belief under the dominance of action is what has been called "learning from experience." A particular action successfully demonstrates the falsity of the proposition that no such class of actions exist. Action often dramatically illustrates by inference what can be done. A burned child shuns the fire, and a man who has synthesized a protein in a laboratory has shown that proteins can be synthesized.

Overt activities almost always involve changes in artifacts. By artifacts, I mean those material objects which are altered by human efforts in order to render them more efficient for human uses. And changes in artifacts are not merely one-way effects which end there; they invariably constitute part of an organ-artifact circuit which leads off from the activities of the individual and issues back in effects upon him, with the last stage constituting the first stage of a new cycle. Thus while the individual affects the artifact, it is also true that the artifact affects the individual. Activity occurs in an endless chain which cumulatively has the effect of shifting the body of individual beliefs.

We have looked at beliefs acquired through thought, feeling, and action, but many other grounds for belief exist. Among these are: analogy, authority, common sense, dreams, egotism, emotion, habit, pathology, revelation, tradition. I have omitted one more in order to say a few words about it: consistency. Beliefs are often accepted because they are compatible with other beliefs which are already held. Beliefs may be regarded as kinds of behavior patterns awaiting discharge which can be triggered by external events, but in the meanwhile they are reinforced by other beliefs with which they agree. The internal environment is disturbed by conflicting beliefs but supported by consistent ones. The tendency to establish an order among beliefs is a property of their maintenance.

II

The mind is a function of the body through memory, for memory makes consciousness possible, and without consciousness there could be no deliberate thought. In memory there must be something learned and retained, as, for example, an image and an attitude toward it; in other words, a belief. A memory on this theory becomes a percept or a concept accompanied by belief. The image itself may be of the faint kind that accompanies a concept learned by means of symbols or the strong kind that is learned through sense perception. In either case it must be accepted to some extent, that is to say, believed. What we believe we do not think of as belief but as knowledge: information obtained in the past but not confined to the past in its generality.

Beliefs tend to persist. Degrees of strength of belief may be listed as follows in the order of increasing intensity: a belief of which the subject is not at all sure; one into which he is prepared to inquire further; one on which he is prepared to bet money; one for which he is willing to take greater chances; one on which he may be asked to risk his life; one for which he is ready to die; one which he is incapable of denying; one of which he is unaware; and finally, one of which he cannot be made aware.

Most beliefs are unconsciously held. Every individual has stored in his memory, available for instant recall, two sets of beliefs. One set he has obtained by growing up in a particular society. He is rarely, if ever, aware of how and when he acquired his most fundamental beliefs; there are so many avenues of acquisition, informal as well as formal. He learns as he grows from childhood to adulthood all of the lore on which his society has come traditionally to operate. This is what I have elsewhere described as the public retention schema, public because they are shared. A public retention schema is a system of social beliefs which can issue at any time as rules of behavior, but which in the meanwhile function to determine how the individual in conformity with the other members of his society feels about things.

But there is also in every individual a private set of beliefs which he has acquired as a result of his own peculiar encounters and development. Every individual lives a life to some extent, however small, which is different from the lives of those around him, and this segment accounts for his private beliefs, private because they are *not* shared. This is the private retention schema.

The private schema is peculiar to a given individual; the public schema is one which he holds in common with all the members of his culture. Together they constitute the total body of his beliefs.

One task which must be performed by every individual is to reconcile these two sets of beliefs. If his private set differs markedly from the public set, then he is either a genius or a fool: an individual who cannot meet the demands of his society or one who chooses to rise above them.

Absolute belief is called faith. Beliefs less than absolute have to be supported by evidence, whereas faith is belief without evidence. An unreasonable belief is also a faith; Tertullian advised, "Believe that which is absurd." Faith is comforting, and the difficulty arises that all faiths are equally comforting. There is no criterion in this respect for choosing between faiths; which makes of belief the cheapest thing in the world, since it does not matter which one is held. Everybody can have one. The truth of beliefs does not have to be known to the believer; indeed, beliefs may be stronger when the truth is *not* known. One believes in something, not in the knowledge of it. Belief is a feeling that looks straight through to the object of belief, without the evidential intermediation of knowledge.

With repetition, belief becomes more firmly entrenched; ritual reinforces it. In religious observances, the consummatory response of belonging, with its ritual repetition, becomes a need-terminating affair. The faraway object promising permanence — either the whole universe or the cause of it — calls for identification, which means the subject losing himself in the object, becoming, as it were, immersed. Religious belief looks to the goal of surviving death.

III

The final outcome of thought of whatever variety, then, is a network of beliefs, the retention schemata. They are stored in the memory where they are available to releasing mechanisms. The function of such mechanisms is to connect up events with the relevant beliefs. Not all beliefs, of course, lead directly to action. All are prepared to do so, but not all are called out by relevant events. And it often happens that the making of a connection is the occasion for an unconscious, taxis-controlled act: impulsive behavior, we are inclined to call it. More usually, the releasing mechanism takes the form of a deliberate decision which is called the will and results from a kind of rule of inference operating between theorematic beliefs and the field of overt behavior.

Beliefs are felt thoughts, and they lead to action. The impulse to action is always there in virtue of the existence of skeletal muscles. They constitute an imbalance and an irritation, a painful dispositional state. Equilibrium can be restored only by the appropriate action. Thus decisions are relief mechanisms designed to facilitate the evacuation of surplus emotional content. There is, in short, a need to act; based on belief and triggered by the will, the muscles respond by effecting environmental changes. These in turn react back on the body of beliefs.

All beliefs lead to aggressions of some sort resulting in alterations in the environment. These tend to be constructive, but where actions are frustrated, they turn violent and destructive. If the individual is not allowed to do what he or she believes should be done, then he or she will back away only to come at it in another fashion, only this time the effects of his or her actions will be quite different. Always, however, belief is involved.

IV

Belief is supported by social pressure. It requires strength of mind and character to deny a truth everyone else seems to accept. Original thinkers are often at odds with their societies. As I have pointed out already, the difficulty is that those who cannot meet the social demands that are made on them share with those who can but do not choose to do so an equal divergence from the established norms. The genius and the fool have much in common, and the genius more often than not must bear the opprobrium of being regarded as a fool. If he or she was right in his opinions, he or she may or may not live to see them adopted by the majority.

The body of beliefs, then, is held in the memory, an old-fashioned name for the unconscious. The deeper the level of the unconscious, the more primitive the level of the qualitative proposition represented by belief, so that anyone endeavoring to think through consciousness to the unconscious will encounter the elements of systems but in reverse: he will move past the stages of inference, reach lower than theorems, and finally get down to the level of the axioms themselves. In the sense that these axioms are common to all the individuals in a culture, they are social.

If the axioms which support the beliefs are social, they are also ontological, where by that term will be meant 'concerned with basic value systems'. Here, then, at the level of unconsciously-held beliefs resides that profoundest of all beliefs, the belief in what is real. By 'real' I mean the immediate object of values.

No individual can live among his fellows for any length of time and share their interests and activities without holding in common with them some beliefs about the ultimate nature of things. These beliefs may be implicit rather than explicit, but they dominate most effectively every one of his thoughts, feelings, and actions. Unconscious beliefs are contained as consequences more clearly in feelings and actions than they are in the expressions of conscious thoughts. And so it is at the level of feeling and action that we readily find the phenomenon of the concrete ontology. A man or woman may defend one belief and yet, under the pressure of a critical situation, act out quite another. The axiomatic nature of our most fundamental beliefs is carefully concealed. The less he or she is aware of them, the more strongly they operate. Beliefs in this sense function as delayed responses; they are the axioms dictating behavior. The culturally prevalent, concrete ontology, as held in the unconscious, is the greatest force in the life of every individual.

I cannot leave this topic without mentioning the question of doubt. Everyone has a great store of knowledge, and the ignorant no less than the well-informed. The only difference is that the 'knowledge' of the ignorant is apt to be false. A false belief is not a belief in what is false, but a belief in what is true which happens to be false. When difficulties appear to the believer in what he holds to be true, doubt arises.

Doubt, the opposite of belief, is an interim affair, but it can replace belief in the service of inquiry. Belief is shaken only when conflicts or contradictions appear. Contradictions in the retention schemata are found either between elements of the schemata or between those elements and external theories or facts. Doubt is always based on conflicting material. This conflict has to be resolved in the foreground and the issue returned to the background. Doubt is self-liquidating and always has a short life expectancy.

Doubt has fewer social consequences than belief, except in those cases where doubt calls for refraining from action. The sceptic, the doubter, has only demonstrated another and more alien set of beliefs, for he cannot exist without beliefs of some sort. However, in the name of doubt, many positive steps have been taken. Doubt does not turn the individual away from action; it turns him to other actions which, were it not for the doubt, he would never have taken.

CHAPTER III

THE PRAGMATIC
THEORY OF KNOWLEDGE

All philosophers know about Peirce and many have read his work, yet his reputation still falls somewhat short of what it should be in the case of a full-scale figure. For he is hardly known at all outside of professional circles. The shortcomings can be softened somewhat if we remember that in the United States at the present time, there are no truly famous native philosophers; there is no such thing as an American philosopher whose name is a household word as so many are in Europe. Not even our best novelists acknowledge philosophers as influences; Zen Buddhists, perhaps, but philosophers seldom, if ever. The best known American names in philosophy are those of William James and John Dewey, but neither was known popularly for his philosophy; James made his reputation in psychology, and Dewey made his in education.

Peirce did not present his philosophy in a comprehensive system, although he made plans to do so more than once. The question of whether he had a system, in other words whether or not such a plan could have been carried out, has been left open. Many investigators have supported the idea that Peirce did have a system, while as many others have insisted that he did not. Can the truth of this question be credited absolutely only on one side or the other? There is a sense in which a system has a constrictive as well as a liberative effect, and perhaps a man would be ill-advised to put the finishing touches to such an enterprise until he was sure he had nothing more to say. Those who consider systems of philosophy to be outdated and who consequently would save Peirce from what they view as a false charge perhaps do not understand what they are admitting, for a system is only another way of talking about consistency. It might be fair to ask why empirical-minded philosophers feel on more secure grounds with piecemeal work, as though Rutherford had been an empiricist and Einstein not, when in fact there is more than one way of doing science: the grand theorist is as much a scientist as the patient investigator, and the same can be said for philosophers.

The question probably hangs on whether Peirce in the course of his long life abandoned his earlier ideas for later ones or merely developed the earlier ideas. Very likely, no clear case can be made for either. A man not only adds to his work during the course of a long lifetime, he also develops it, and in the development significant changes may occur so that in the end his position has altered. Thus it has come about in Peirce's case that some scholars look for his system, while others think it more important to follow the course of his development.

A thinker's reputation grows in proportion not only to the number of citations and references to his work in journal articles and books by his professional colleagues, but also to the degree of divergence of the views of those who seek to derive from him, until it begins to appear almost as though fame (as Rilke said) consists in a sufficient number of misunderstandings. But the appearances in this instance could be wrong.

It is a measure of the size of Peirce as an influence that his shadow nonetheless lies broadly across the American intellectual scene, and he still stands there, a large and powerful but lonely thinker, awaiting full recognition. It is discouraging to consider that had he been German, there would by now be a Peirce *Gesellschaft* and a leading Peirceian scholar in every institution of higher learning. But all is not over, and the best may yet be ahead. After all, there is our Society, and there is a journal, and, even if *The Transactions* to stay afloat has had to open its pages to the study of the work of other men, it does exist.

At the present time, most American philosophers go to Europe for guidance, to Wittgenstein's followers in England, to the memory of Kierkegaard and Husserl on the Continent, and, in our own day, to Heidegger and Sartre. The sin is one of omission rather than of commission: no one would want to make the chauvinistic point that productivity should begin at home and remain there, but at least it should be found at home also, as in fact it was once in the days of Peirce and James, of Royce and Mead.

Philosophy is indeed the last of the great cultural enterprises in which we still look exclusively abroad. Culturally speaking, this is at best an unhealthy situation. Let us hope that it will not last. If we turn back to see the work of Peirce as a whole and try to understand the direction in which it points, we may find one kind of corrective, for Peirce was sure, if he was sure of anything, that the direction of philosophy was toward open-ended inquiry, with no absolutes to render it unnecessary and no preconceptions to bar the way. He refused to abandon metaphysics in order to gain empiricism because he thought that empiricism has its own metaphysics, and so he endeavored to explain empiricism and discover its metaphysics.

If we can feel inspiration in Peirce to locate the roots of a fresh philosophical enterprise in our own already impressive cultural achievement, even though what we emerge with might not resemble too closely his own ideas and values, it would still owe much to the spirit of his undertakings and in this sense continue what he so courageously started. Grounding research in Peirce's writings still leaves open the prospect of interpolation as well as extrapolation. There are fields in which he did not excel, such as aesthetics, and others with which he was not concerned, such as politics and economics, How would a Peirceian politics be constructed? Again, in those fields in which he did do important work, his ideas could be extended. To the philosopher who possesses the ideal combination of a rigorous training and a flexible yet controlled imagination, the future is wide. It is probably the case that nothing has been done for the last time, and so very much not even for the first time.

But surely the greatest monument to Peirce that could be erected in these days of narrow, if deep, investigations and intense professional intolerances would be not only to say but to mean what he advocated, to leave all doors open to inquiry. One measure of a culture is the extent to which its leading advocates are able not only to welcome differences of opinion but even to encourage them and to assist in their promulgation. Unhappily, this is far from the case now.

Ours is the day of the preeminence of experimental science and of the fine arts and literature, but not of philosophy. Philosophy is a neglected field, and a neglected field is a shrinking field, in which everyone feels crowded and unhappy. Philosophers, like other people, need living space; but since it is a philosophical living space, they are the only ones who can provide it for each other. It was not something Peirce enjoyed in his own day but it was something he advocated with enthusiasm, and it can be counted among the good things he has left us. We will be doing him honor if we strike out with imagination in every hopeful direction, in search of the truths which the cardinal axiom of his faith always assumed were there to be found.

Progress in philosophy does get interrupted at times. Other activities are going on in human life which often obscure philosophical inquiry and cause us to forget some of the best ideas of the greatest thinkers. But progress does catch up. Let me give a large example.

You will recall the studies of Descartes, Spinoza, and Leibniz, who thought that reliable knowledge could be obtained by the method of reasoning, and the work of Locke, Berkeley, and Hume, who looked primarily to sense experience. if man has three capacities, which are for thought, feeling, and action, then we have one left to examine: action.

The effort to place activity on a respectable philosophical footing was pursued by Peirce into the construction of a metaphysics. He recognized as its primary categories: quality or firstness, reaction or secondness, and relation or thirdness. Secondness is reaction (6.32); it is the "brute actions of one subject or substance on another" (5.469), and "action, actuality is ... one element of phenomena" (1.419). It may be described as "force in its widest sense" (1.487).

To the names of the men who relied on reasoning as a source of reliable knowledge, and to those who relied in a corresponding way on sense experience, we must add the three who relied on activity: Peirce, James, and Dewey. Pragmatism, initiated by Peirce, supplied the missing third capacity of the human pursuit of reliable knowledge.

This third method has turned out to be the most powerful of all, for it includes and subordinates the other two. And it does so because it is the method of science itself, which employs all three capacities in their proper order, shifting from the domination of one to the domination of the other, until an approximation of the truth stands revealed.

Peirce was a philosopher with a strong interest in the method of the physical sciences. His philosophy was colored by his interest. He tried to make a parallel of the scientific method for use in philosophy. He did not quite succeed, but he did succeed in discovering a new approach to philosophical problems.

What concerned Peirce was linking theory and practice by relating the theory of philosophy to the practice of everyday life. Philosophy, in this relation, was represented by truth. The way to discover truth was by using the scientific method, the laboratory method of experiment, and the field method of close observation.

Peirce was on the track of something basic. He was trying to discover the source of reliable knowledge and thought he had found it in the scientific method. In that method, action is the leading edge. Observations and experiments are usually conducted with complex instruments involving many kinds of planned moves, which means that every observation and every experiment requires activity. But since the capacities for feeling and thought are also involved, the scientific method is one that calls out all of the capacities of the entire man. It is the whole man engaged in inquiry. The search for a theory of reliable knowledge seems to have arrived home at last.

Once a truth is discovered, the next step is to put it into practice. The truth is what works best in practice, and so from the point of view of practice itself, it is best to discover the truth. *What is true will work.* This was Peirce's pragmatic declaration.

But that is not the end of the story. William James tried hard to understand Peirce's philosophy and to adopt it. But he did not underatand it fully, and so he adopted something like it, which he, too, called *pragmatism.* But James' version of pragmatism was sharply different from Peirce's. Although he used the same words to describe it, he used them in a different order. Where Peirce had said that *what is true will work,* James declared that *what works is true.*

Words are very trickly things; it is more difficult than we think to make them say exactly what we mean, no more, no less. Although the two statements sound very much alike, they are quite different in meaning since the one does not convert into the other, and so it should not be too surprising that they led to sharply different kinds of behavior. For Peirce's version led to the scientific laboratory where laws are discovered; James' version led to the exigencies of industry.

You may remember what the frontier in the western states was like toward the end of the last century. You have seen it in many a movie and read about it in many a novel. Justice was administered in very rough ways. The pioneers were too busy carving a civilization out of the forests and open plains to have time for the niceties of morality. The important thing was to get on with the business at hand. In short, they had a philosophy of practice, although they did not have any words for it. James, without meaning to, gave them the words. Never mind about truth as such, he seemed to be saying, "if it works it is true." Stick to workability, in other words, and the truth will take care of itself.

This may serve very well for a frontier philosophy and yet not do quite as well for a settled civilization. The influence of the western frontier was felt strongly by those living more conventional lives in the eastern states. It might have misled them if they had followed it too faithfully. Business men always did accept it, but there were others with less special interests who did not.

In the 1920s when Mussolini's "fascists" were in control of the government of Italy, many things that had not worked so well before were made to work for the first time. American business men came back from vacations in Italy, and remarked, "You can say what you like about Mussolini, but he has got the trains running on time."

The pragmatic viewpoint appealed to the "practical-minded man," who was chiefly concerned with the problems of the present moment. The only trouble was that a philosophy which seemed to be working well for the short run did not work for the long run. And it was not many years before pragmatic considerations led Mussolini to take his fancies into an international war, which neither he nor they could handle. He ended up hanging by his heels next to his mistress when he was caught by anti-fascist patriots while trying to escape to Germany.

The trouble with the pragmatism of the short run, James' pragmatism, was that it did not spell out the number of trials needed to assure "workability." As a quick check on the truth of a statement, James' short run version of pragmatism is no help, for it could just as easily give a wrong answer as a right one. How long a time do we need before we can be sure that something works and is therefore a "truth"? Peirce had said what is true will work, but he, too, had not spelled out the length of time that would be necessary in order to be sure that the number of trials was sufficient to guarantee a truth.

Like all good scientists, Peirce wished to leave this an open question. Scientists hold all their conclusions, their "laws" and their "facts," forever open to question and subject to revision. Like the ancient Greek skeptics and Stoics, Peirce preferred to talk in terms of percentages rather than in terms of certainties, in terms of the probable truth rather than the "absolute truth." The probable we can know from experience; the absolute as such we can never know.

This difference led Peirce to set up within his philosophy a principle which he called *fallibilism.* That is to say, he held out always the possibility that whatever he said might be wrong. A principle of error was necessary in order to avoid making claims that might be too sweeping.

James missed the point that there are intermediate steps between theory and practice, and so he thought that metaphysical theories have no application. But Peirce knew better than that, and we have had since then many elaborate examples of the thesis that James was wrong. Look at the tremendous effects of the metaphysical theory of dialectical materialism and you will see that the more abstract the theory, the greater its effects upon practice, once a path has been found leading from one to the other.

Dewey, the last of the three great pragmatists, made the mistake, which Peirce would never have made, of bringing the subject back into the picture, thus insuring that his theory of reality would have to be deduced from his theory of knowledge. Peirce, remember, had defined reality as externality. But for Dewey both the subject and the object of knowledge are swallowed up by "experience" which, so to speak, makes them both possible. "Experience" was a key word for Dewey as it had been for Kant, and it led to further studies in epistemology, not to the hypothetico-experimental method of the physical sciences, and so ended, for the philosophers at least, a new direction in the study of activity which had looked at first to be so engaging. The rest of the story has been told by the scientists.

CHAPTER IV

THE EXPANDED ENVIRONMENT

I

The immediate environment, to anyone who takes the time to reflect on it, cannot be explained on its own. Experiences demand to be sorted out. The individual, in the course of pursuing his daily life, receives a number of sense impressions and ideas, and as he moves about encounters both assistance toward his goals, and obstacles placed in the way of them. In ordinary events, he is bound to notice that there are similarities and differences; most of these will be trivial but some will be crucial, and all will occur in a more or less jumbled up fashion. Solving immediate practical problems, which arise when he picks his way among the objects in his environment, must occupy the forefront of his conscious mind, but if he pauses long enough to contemplate what lies ahead of him in the larger picture, he will be led to speculate in general on what-there-is, and he might even try to put together a comprehensive account that will temporarily, at least, satisfy his curiosity. This is the practical side of metaphysics.

Starting from the thinnest wisp of existence: a passing thought, perhaps, or a fleeting glance, he might be able to surmise that everything is connected in some way — differences obscurely, similarities more obviously — and so end with a theory of the whole world. And precisely there is where philosophy begins for the average individual. Presumably, he will have noted or had called to his attention that while both similarities and differences prove their reality to him by offering surprises and resistance, the similarities recur while the differences perish, a most intriguing contrast which he will want explained. Thus there arises in his thoughts the possibility of constructing a permanent conception which can be interpreted in modified form to describe whatever occurs, provided only that the area of difference be fleshed out with accidental elements and colorful details. Philosophy, in a word, has had its origins in the search for order.

A little knowledge of early philosophy will remind our individual that what he regards as similarities have been noted to have certain properties in common: they are abstract, indestructible, and completely general. Plato called them "Ideas" and regarded them as independent both of the minds which know them and of the material particulars in which they are exemplified; since the Middle Ages, they have been named "universals."

Similarly, differences exist in the world where they constitute the characteristics of substances — we should say "matter" now, although Aristotle used both terms. All material things are marked by differences — every material thing is in some sense unique — and all of them perish.

Thus our individual has recovered for himself the truth contained in Plato's "universals" and Aristotle's "matter." These are the two domains in which he lives, in which he has thoughts and feelings, and in which he acts. That is to say, he lives in the world of matter but is answerable to the conditions provided by universals. The domain of matter seems to be the base line, but control over it has to be made in terms of its regularities as defined by universal law.

On some reflection, it becomes evident that the truth about both universals and substance is exceedingly complex, and now we know that we must explore the first as the domain of abstractions and the second as the world of matter and radiation, to say nothing of the connections between them. It is an enormous task which has only been begun, and the reason for this is not far to seek. The realism of both Plato and Aristotle has been under attack for so long that its adherents have been kept busy defending it and could not spare the time to make the necessary explorations.

Thanks to the progress in science our individual has learned a lot about both of these domains, which are far more complex than had been supposed, for both prove to be many-layered. The question of which is the more real does not occur because there is equality of being: all is equally real. The sciences have been occupied with exploring the material world, discovering its laws, and expressing them in the language of mathematics which belongs to the domain of universals, Perhaps it would be best to look at each of these domains separately.

II

First, then, the domain of universals. This is a completely abstract affair, in which the following are to be found in an hierarchy:

1) mathematics and logic
2) universal terms and qualities
3) relations and forces
4) propositions and scientific laws

1) The mathematical entities are true and hold without exception, for example, 1,2,3...n, considered as ranges of reference. Similarly with the logic of 'if p, then q' which, like mathematics, is true, but only in the abstract domain, not in the world of matter. '2+2»' holds inexorably, but only with abstract objects, not with material objects. In the world of matter, 2 raindrops + 2 raindrops might equal 1 (large) raindrop, so that here '2+2=1'!

2) Next after the layer of mathematical and logical entities comes the layer of universal terms, which name classes of material things, of individual substances, such as 'chair', 'planet', 'man'. The individuals themselves belong to the world of matter, not to the domain of universals, but their classes do belong to the world of matter, and such classes only when they are non-denumerable. A finite class is not a universal, only a collection of material things having a close resemblance to one another. But when the members of a class can not be enumerated because they do not come to an end, then it is an universal class.

Qualities are universals, though perhaps not obviously so. A blue rubber ball might be destroyed, and that particular ball will not exist again, but the 'blue' will, for there could always be other objects of the same shade of blue. And the same can be said for any qualities.

3) Relations connect two or more objects, '— to the left of —' connects two objects; 'a is darker than either b or c' connects three objects; and so on. Like qualities, relations cannot be destroyed and

may always recur. But relations have a wider range of application than qualities, because qualities are found only among material objects whereas relations exist also among logical and mathematical objects. The relation 'larger than,' for instance, applies to abstract numbers, as when it is said that '10 is larger than 9', or to material things, as when it is said that 'Tom is larger than Harry'.

Forces are relations. They connect two objects, and the connections in this case can be quantified; what changes the state of motion or rest of a body can be measured. Force is also qualitative, as must be evident to anyone who has ever felt pressure on the surface of the skin. They also exist independently. Force, in short, represents a set of abstract conditions which, like all abstractions, can be exemplified in the domain of matter. The fact that when force is active it involves material objects, has led some investigators to doubt its status as a relation, but as relations are universals, so forces are qualities, which should put their doubts to rest.

4) Next below the universals in the order of descending generality comes the layer of universal propositions. These connect universals: parts with other parts, parts with wholes, and wholes with other wholes. The familiar 'All men are mortal' is a universal proposition. The layer of universal propositions is especially important because it includes the scientific laws: Newton's familiar law of gravitation is an obvious example of a universal proposition.

Because scientific laws are often used in a practical way to control concrete fact, their abstract nature is often forgotten. Newton's law of gravitation is stated for a vacuum, a condition which cannot be reached in the world of matter. It can be availed of only by substituting approximations, for in itself it is completely general.

The many-layered domain of universals can be described as an abstract affair, not because men have abstracted the knowledge of it (though they have), but rather because it *is* abstract, which is to say, removed from and independent of the world of matter and always available for discovery. The elements of the abstract domain are important, not because men have found them by abstracting from the similarities of material objects, but rather because they are more reliable, not subject to change with time, as the material objects themselves are. The triangle is still what it was in Euclid's day.

Elements of the abstract domain are not only removed from time, they are equally removed from space, since they apply equally to all of space. When we come down through the abstract layers, we find the applications more restricted. Any two things can constitute a pair, but two horses do not equal two sheep and only in a limited sense two other horses. The minute we touch down at matter, we find ourselves confined to particular classes. But we are thus far only touching down, not remaining there for a longer inspection.

I should point out that each of these layers is subdivided. For instance, mathematics is structured into algebra, analysis, and topology, though with the underpinning of mathematical logic. All are abstract, but this does not mean that some are not more abstract than others. A good example is Cantor's transfinite arithmetic, in which some infinites are subsumed by others.

III

I have been describing the structure of the abstract domain of universals and endeavoring to outline the character of its various layers. It will be best at this point to turn to a description of the domain of matter.

Matter, and I should also add energy, exists in time and space, as universals do not. In the material world are found the elements of order but largely out of order, and as a consequence, they are engaged in interacting constructively and destructively.

That is why the world is what it has been called: a busy buzzing confusion, and why violence is so prevalent at all levels, physical as well as social. Natural laws are the indications of regularity in the world, for some apply continually wherever matter exists, such as the law of gravitation, while others can be brought into play at any date and place only if the material circumstances call them out, such as the electrolysis of water. Things which have been removed from their rightful place in some order struggle to get back, and in so doing, encounter resistance which they endeavor to overcome. The results are, as one might have expected, a mixture of elements or of various forms of energy, whether it is one mass exerting a physical force upon another mass or one man seeking to influence the actions of others.

What exists, then, is a partial order which is the world of material existence, and which is highly structured. It has been named the integrative levels and consists in organizations of material objects and forces, as these are found to be primarily physical, chemical, biological, psychological, or cultural. There are the broad headings, but each one is subdivided. The physical, for example, begins with quarks; above them are the elementary particles, next the atoms, then the molecules and the macromolecules. Each level has its own characteristic kind of energy: radiation at the physical level, valence at the chemical, awareness at the psychological, life at the biological, the ethos at the cultural.

We can see, then, that each of the integrative levels is composed of aggregations of elements of the level just below, plus one emergent quality. It takes a great many atoms to make a molecule, a great many molecules to make a cell, a great many cells to make an organism, and a great many organisms to make a society. Thus there is a dependence of the higher on the lower, but also, and conversely, a determination of the lower by the higher. The result is a complex structure.

The integrative levels present a deceptively neat picture of the way material objects are organized and the way in which they logically belong, as deduced from their separate but related organizations. That is, however, emphatically not the way in which they present themselves in the material world. There is no indication that they come and go, for all are finite and enjoy short lives. Some last longer than others — an atom may last much longer than a man — but all come into existence at some date and place, and all perish. While they exist, some increase, while others disintegrate; so that the situation at any point-instant is a fluid affair, the result of many types of energy playing upon one another.

IV

We have been looking at some of the details of both the domain of universals and the world of material existence. Now we must see how they are related. It has been noted that they are made into a whole in certain peculiar ways. The knowledge of the domain of universals has come from an acquaintance with the world of particulars. Order has been preserved by abstracting from conflict and, above all, from chance, both of which characterize material existence, for the domain of universals contains ideals, perfections, completions; while the particulars in the world of matter struggle with disorder, chance, imperfections, and, above all, strivings. The task of studying the relations between universals and material objects has been undertaken by epistemology and by the scientific method.

In epistemology, the question is answered of how the knowledge of the domain of universals is obtained. The answer involves a process of abstracting from material particulars to the general classes to which they belong. The individual who perceives how much individual horses have in common — more in fact than their differences — arrives at the concept of 'horse' as a class governing not only his past experience of such objects, but also all future ones. He learns about abstract objects, such as universals, by the process of discerning the typicality of particulars; only it must be borne in mind that the universals so discovered have features not present in the process. Consider the perfection and the imperishability of the abstraction 'horse,' which are not true of any particular horse nor of any finite collection of horses. There is known to be an 'inductive leap' in the course of gaining general knowledge from particular experiences, which marks off the former from the latter.

It is crucial to the theory of what-there-is to remember always that what we know is not dependent upon our knowing; quite the reverse, in fact. This is the mistake made by subjectivists, who forget that were there no object, there could be no knowledge of it, whereas there could be such an object without the knowledge. Indeed, the progress of learning about hitherto unknown objects is clear evidence that more exists to be known than is known at any one time.

How is our knowledge of scientific laws obtained? In a word, how do we learn about universals from the study of matter? Full abstraction discloses that there is only one scientific method. Although its employment in the separate experimental sciences is always mediated by external circumstances, essentially the same set of procedures, conducted in approximately the same order, can be uncovered in laboratory practices. The scientific method of investigation is an ongoing process which lends itself to analysis into seven well-defined stages. These stages are: observation, induction, hypothesis, experiment, calculation, prediction, and control. Observations are made in order to uncover provocative facts. Inductions from the provocative facts are made with a view to discovering hypotheses worthy of investigation. This is the stage of brilliant originative insights.

The hypotheses in this fashion are then set up for testing in four ways. The first way is the one peculiar to science and involves the use of experiments. In the second, the hypothesis is matched against existing laws by means of mathematical calculations. The third way is to make predictions from the hypothesis and to test it against the relevant events. The fourth way is to employ the hypothesis — now usually called a theory — to exercise control over practice. Those hypotheses which pass all four tests are considered to be established, always tentatively, of course, as scientific laws.

V

Our individual presumably has been looking with us at the broad features of what there is, as set forth in the two domains of universals and material existence. Now it might be helpful if against this background, we were to examine with him the special case of the human species.

It will be necessary to blow up the importance of the highest of the integrative levels because of an obviously special interest. The level of the cultural is where man with all of his works exists, and our individual will have found that this is where he belongs and has his peculiar niche.

Man himself occupies a position at the highest of the integrative levels, which is the cultural, though he himself is composed of elements of all the levels below. In addition, he has brought about a new situation, for we must count with him at the cultural level all the artifacts: those items which he has made by altering material objects until they take the forms which are useful to him. A culture is an organization of human individuals together with the artifacts and their effects on him.

Man stands in the middle of his material culture, thanks to the rapidly accelerating discoveries in the physical sciences, and finds that he is confronted with an expanded environment in a vastly larger and more complex world than he had formerly been led to believe. At the level of ordinary awareness and encountering only those gross objects available to his unaided senses, his position is suddenly challenged.

There have been posited two distinct orders of being: a domain of universals and a world of matter. The domain of universals is governed by the laws of logic. Matter exists in time and space; governed by the ordinary world it should henceforth be called the mesocosmos, because recently man has become aware that he occupies a position in the middle between the many-layered world of the very small, the microcosmos, on the down side; and the many-layered world of the very large, the macrocosmos, on the up side. On the down side are those small material objects he encounters only through instruments, such as the microscope, and on the up side are those large ones he also knows only through instruments, such as the optical telescope.

So much for the elements of the partial order making up the world of matter. The total picture is much more complicated because of the fact that the elements are mostly out of order. This occasions the additional factor of conflicts which occur by chance. And chance is brought about by the intersection of causal laws introducing conflicting elements of order, and is thus an authentic ingredient, and not merely a subjective fraction or illusion.

The situation in which man finds himself has both elements of order (the integrative levels) and disorder (the ongoing struggle of all material things in time and space to survive and, perhaps, to increase, despite the conflicts and oppositions).

The human individual, just as we might expect, is a material object working to reduce its needs. What are these, and to which domain do they belong?

I think we can distinguish two sorts of needs: those which are importunate and those which are important; that is to say, those which are concerned with immediate survival and those which are concerned with ideals. Both sorts are organ-specific, for the organism as a whole works through separate organs, but let us consider them in their proper order: first, those which have to do with survival.

These are needs which trigger drives to discover materials in the immediate environment. Some organs, such as the heart and the vascular system, are obviously internal; they serve the organism as a whole; but others are directly related to substances in the environment. The tissues need water, the stomach food, sex a mate. These are pressing needs, and if they are not reduced, the individual does not do well. The organ which serves immediate survival is the skin: 'save the surface and you save all', the advertisement says, and it is true of the skin which signals injury when penetration is threatened.

And now the set of needs having to do with ideals: those involving curiosity, security, and activity. These are needs having a longer range, not matters of immediate attention: the needs to know, to be, and to do. The need to know is reduced when the drive for knowledge succeeds. The brain, in short, 'needs' information. The need to be calls out the skin again, though this time in a more remote connection. Not immediate survival, but what may be described as long-range survival, is also served by the skin, but this time when it comes into direct contact with a symbol of the universe or its ultimate cause: kissing the black stone at Mecca for the Muslims, the sacraments for the Roman Catholics. In more primitive religions, symbolic security through skin contact has a long history; there it is known as "contagious magic," and serves the same purpose in much the same way.

The individual lives at once, then, at all of the integrative levels: he has a physical mass and force, a chemical constitution, a biological organism, a psychological capacity, and a certain set of cultural beliefs which he entertains while operating a certain set of artifacts. And he lives in an environment which is similarly layered: a physical environment, consisting of the earth with its atmosphere and light from the sun; a chemical environment of which these objects are composed; a biological environment of organisms from bacteria to plants and animals and other humans; and a cultural environment in which his own culture struggles to compete with other cultures. No one has yet worked out the formulas to deal with so many variables.

At this point, it is possible that our individual will note that in addition to singular conceptions, he has to deal with a number of subordinate orders which already seem to be in place. Others like himself evidently had already combined to establish social institutions intended to serve a number of individuals and having a large measure of semipermanence: governments and the like, including that special institution, whatever it is, in which the individual's own professional life is lived. Could he have failed to note also, at this time, that some of these institutions belong to a kind of super-group; for instance, if he is employed in a manufacturing company, that there are other varieties of industry, or if he is in an art such as music, that there are other varieties of art?

Surely he could not have failed to notice also, if his speculations had continued, that all of these super-groups were themselves combined in a still larger group which for want of a better name can be called a state, and if still larger, a civilization. And if he was astute enough to note that there have been different and even rival civilizations, he would want to know as a last inquiry what accounts for the cohesion and degree of consistency that marks all of the enterprises and activities of a civilization.

VI

Our individual would probably recognize by this time that finally he was dealing with an underpinning of assumptions which can be called a philosophy; not one in the form in which it is recognized by professionals, but in the form in which it is concretely imbedded in human culture.

What I have been setting forth in the previous sections is the outline of such philosophy. Such comprehensive accounts have been attacked on the grounds that they could not be proved. That is true; but the reason why is not well understood; and it is not understood either that there might be other reasons for accepting them just the same.

A philosophy presented as a system in order to be complete, must be wholly comprehensive; there cannot be anything outside the system if it is an authentic system. However, there is no way in which it can contain its own proof. Yet if the proof were to lie outside the system, then it could not be regarded as a system of philosophy, which preforce must be complete. Thus there is a genuine contradiction in the very idea of proving a system of philosophy.

The assumptions of a philosophy are contained in its metaphysics. Similarly, but with important differences, a metaphysics cannot be proved, either. For if what has been argued here is in fact the case, namely, that every concrete metaphysics is found to consist in the assumptions of some culture, then where there are rival cultures, each metaphysics assumed by a culture is as true as the workings of that culture allows and requires. And of course there are in fact rival cultures, which means that each culture is 'true' to the extent that it is a pragmatic success and false otherwise, and that its assumptions must possess at least a limited truth.

Thus a philosophy may be accepted as authentic on a *pro tem* basis, which means as the truth insofar as it is known and considered workable and viable until a superior version is discovered. There is no such thing as a complete human culture, only those which are more complete than others. The larger the culture and the more valuable its arts, the more knowledgeable its sciences, and the more complex and efficient its artifacts, then the wider its truth and hence the more acceptable.

Remember that both facts and laws are involved in the notion of truth: true to fact, as well as true to theory. Truth is not merely a matter of consistency; it is also a matter of correspondence, and this means correspondence with all of the known facts. Now it must be obvious that not all of the facts are known and, perhaps, never will be. The sciences are engaged in discovering new facts and new laws every day. Given our knowledge of the immense extent of the material universe in space and time, it is certain that the whole of truth may never be known.

Meanwhile, the individual has a craving for knowledge, which means for truths of theory and truths of fact, which must somehow be satisfied. It can be satisfied to some extent even if only to some extent only, as much, you might say, as anything else in a material existence where the only absolutes are those of logic and mathematics. The knowledge of these last two was derived from the world of matter and can be referred back to it, but never on any absolute basis, never with the absolute certainty to which they apply in their own domain, which is why, of course, a separate domain had to be posited in the first place. Our individual can be certain of the truths of logic and mathematics, but not of their applicability to the material world.

Thus philosophies must rest on plausibility, and can be accepted only to the extent of their explanatory value. We need to know how things fit together, and nothing less than a comprehensive philosophy will perform that task.

VII

The important issue of the practicality of philosophy has been very much confused and misrepresented. If it means the self-conscious and deliberate use of philosophy by professionals, then it has a limited applicability; but it can and indeed does mean much more than that. To understand this point, it will be necessary to refer again to the conception of cultures.

The variety of individuals has been recognized as a natural phenomenon, and so has the variety of societies. It is well known that there are many different ways in which anything can be done: obtaining food, making love, waging war. But what is not as well known is the fact that what is done in a particular way, rather than in any other, discloses the implicit acceptance of a set of abstract ideas.

Every cultural region has its own axioms and behaves in accordance with them, so that when Asians and Africans act differently from Europeans and Americans, it is not difficult to understand why: Indians have learned to live with native contradictions, Africans with unstable and instant changes. Every society is such as it must be, given the established beliefs of its individuals collectively and the possibilities set by the conditions of its physical and biological environment.

But if societies are natural phenomena, so are their foundations; what accounts for the unity and the cohesiveness of societies are their philosophical underpinnings: the unacknowledged yet nonetheless effective assumptions which lie at their base. Thus philosophies are forces of nature rather than systems of beliefs arbitrary and consciously established, natural forces which are as stubborn as any other and which must be recognized and coped with as such. This is both an important point and a new conception, and much follows from it: philosophy raised to a new eminence.

Thus the question of the practicality of philosophy becomes one of the efficiency with which it can be met and engaged; just as true of philosophy as it is of oil in the ground, hurricanes, or any other feature which represents a potential aid or threat to neighboring societies. In a word, if we are to understand the effectiveness of philosophy, we must learn how to think objectively rather than subjectively as we have done for so long. Philosophy, as it exists in men's minds (and I do not deny its residence there also), consists of such ideas as are suggested to them by what they are able to elicit from the environment.

Thinkers do go further, of course: they compare philosophies, and they even think of possible alternatives; this much is mental, and to that extent, the tradition has been helpful. But it has been allowed to obscure the fact that what men have elicited, contrasted, and used as aids to the imaginative constructions which they have entertained is only a small part of what-there-is actually existing in societies and what has surfaced there, served its turn, and later been abandoned.

It may be helpful to end by showing one instance of a cultural philosophy. What better laboratory sample could there be than to

consider the assumptions of the culture of classic Greece? In the fifth
century B.C., there were two religions native to the culture: one rested
on the gods of the Olympic pantheon which the Hellenes seem to have
brought with them when they conquered the native population, the
other on the chthonic deities which the native population already
possessed: Orpheus, the Delphic Oracle, and the like. In a word, the
sky gods represented reason and the earth gods represented material
existence. The Greeks were careful to balance the two and to render
to each its due, which accounts for their magnificent achievements in
philosophy, literature, and the arts, and also in mathematics and the
sciences. The metaphysical realism which the equal reality of these two
orders implies was just what they needed to power the logical discoveries
they made and the material successes they scored.

It is time to return to our individual with a final word. We saw him
in the beginning observing similarities and differences in the
phenomenal world, and we followed his thinking as he was compelled
by the evidence to expand these ideas into the complexities of
knowledge to which they inevitably led. The net result has been to
grasp something of that vast expanded environment which, as he can
now understand, spreads outward from him to all the complexities of
the integrative levels as he stands in the middle of everything, with
the microworld disclosed by particle physics on the one side and the
macroworld disclosed by astronomy on the other. suddenly, as it were
— for he has all this new knowledge that has been gained in the last
couple of centuries — he knows so much more than any of his ancestors
did, and all of it in one way or another calling for new thoughts, new
feelings, and above all, new actions. The challenge of the modern
world is upon him. How will he respond to it? We can only wait and
see.

CHAPTER V

FORCE AS AN ACTIVE QUALITY

Recent discoveries in astrophysics have disclosed the fact that ours is a violent universe. Most of the matter in it — estimates run as high as 95 percent — is in what is now called the hot plasma state, excited ions, a condition exemplified in our neighborhood by the sun. This leaves a mere 5 percent for solids, liquids, and gasses.

To what new propositions in ontology does the recognition of this important fact commit us? To two, it seems to me; to a first proposition that force is a quality, and to a second that the plasma state is the prevalent form of matter.

There are many places in the universe where there is matter without life, but none where there is life without matter. Despite the prevailing violence, there exist also relatively inactive regions, like the planets, where life sometimes emerges. Man himself exists in one such quiet corner in a universe of exploding stars and colliding galaxies, but even there, it is not always so quiet if you count earthquakes, volcanoes, hurricanes, tornados, and extremes of heat and cold.

From the number of gross changes affected by force, we shall have to acknowledge that it is a cosmic condition, and that even on the surface of the earth it is the entering wedge to the understanding of nature.

Given common experience at any moment, the individual has been under the illusion of a fixed and unchanging environment. This is anything but a true picture. The human species lives in relative quiet, but even the earth is restless; it is only some 4.5 billion years old in a universe estimated to have lasted between 13.5 and 15.5 billion years.[1] Within the last half million years, there have been a dozen advances and retreats of the ice sheet. The last retreat began 70,000 years ago and reached its present stage by 8300 B.C. when civilizations were first starting. Mastodons, mammoths, and large reptiles became extinct some 40,000 to 15,000 years before the present. The dinosaurs lasted for 160 million years, ending some 45 million years ago. In our own time, we have witnessed evidence of continental drift (plate tectonics). We seem to be now 5,000 years into the next ice age, which will end in 119,000 years.[2]

Force may be defined as that physical effect which changes or tends to change the state of rest or motion of a body. It is an active quality. How have the philosophers dealt with it?

The answer, I regret to say, is that for the most part they have not. It is simply astonishing that traditional European philosophy, which was so much concerned with qualities, omitted all consideration of force as a quality, when it is the most prevalent quality even on the surface of the earth. The omission certainly destroys whatever comprehensiveness the consideration of the other qualities may have had. The qualities treated by the seventeenth century empiricists were assumed to be passive. The world as reported by the empirical philosophers of the seventeenth and eighteenth centuries was substantially the same as the one that was described by the rationalists of that period. Whether the knowledge was a product of sense experience or the result of reasoning, the conclusions were similar. But they were never summarized for what they were: the account by a passive individual of his experience in the midst of his passive environment.

The elements of the world so discovered were given in subjective terms, called perceptions and thoughts, and were those of an individual who seldom moved or was moved. His perceptions came from particular senses, chiefly sight and hearing, but also taste and smell. None involved activity of any sort, so that the individual was able to sit perfectly still and yet make all of the required observations. The one exception was suggested by Berkeley, but his differences were negligible and were never extended as they might have been. Locke, Berkeley, and Hume were mostly concerned with this kind of sense experience, and much the same could be said for Descartes, Spinoza, and Leibniz, who put together a rational account of the individual and his world.

The sense perceptions of the empirical philosophers gave rise to the knowledge of qualities, and the thoughts of the corresponding set of rationalists gave rise to the knowledge of relations. Qualities and relations were the units dealt with the most, and it was not noticed that they were as inert as the subjects to whose senses and mind they were supposed to be attached.

Evidently for all of these philosophers the ongoing world of activity and conflict, of constructions and destructions, was only an appearance whose reality was made up of passive units. The mind of the knower was supposed to contribute a considerable portion of what is known, so that in a subjectively-oriented perspective it was considered theoretically possible to inspect the validity of the contents of knowledge by an examination of the workings of the mind.

The shortcomings of idealism were never more in evidence than in the tacit assumption that things are as they are supposed to be. The world was expected to conform to the ideas which were held about it, and nobody bothered to check out the conformity except the scientists, and their conclusions were not admitted to have any bearing on philosophy. The scientists had followed a different path; for whereas the empirical philosophers were occupied with the subjective end of sense experience and so sought in the mind of the subject a clue to the nature of reality, the empirical scientists looked at the objective end and thus landed not in the experience itself, but in what it disclosed to them about the material world. The use by both philosophers and scientists of the term *empiricism* has been to this extent misleading, for they meant quite different things by it.

There was a philosophy of scientific empiricism available, if the philosophers of the time had only known about it. As things turned out, they did not, and the result was not altogether good for philosophy. The lone dissenter was Leibniz, who in a tantalizing fashion had almost seen the point. His world was composed of units of force, called monads; but these were, after all, "windowless" and unaffected by their environment, more like metaphysical components and not the kind of force that is meant when engineers describe what one physical body exerts on another. That the two had anything in common was not at the time suspected by anyone.

How did it happen that the philosophical empiricists of the eighteenth century had overlooked the one important sense organ which held the clue to such a large area of existence? I allude, of course, to the sense of touch. The understanding of the quality of force might have come first from the generalization of the sense of touch, pressures on the skin, as the one sense which is in contact with that element of the world which offers resistance. It might have made more difficult a subjective interpretation, such as that of Locke, for it might have led him to see that the defence of the theory of sense objects, as products of sense organs, had been rendered incomplete. The resistance to touch is not likely to be offered by a substance that is not there and could not long have remained a 'something, we know not what.' In forceful activity, bodies affect each other as well as the knower and do not depend upon being "permanent possibilities of sensation", as Mill had thought they did.

And then again, why was it that no one seems to have noticed that the coordination of the senses — including the sense of touch — produces a conception, not otherwise obtainable, of a world of stereoscopic objects possessed of diverse properties and interacting with each other in bland disregard of the subject? For a material object to be successively seen, touched, smelled, tasted, and collected into a conception of the whole, either it must be moved or the subject must move in relation to it, and in this way some knowledge of it might become available to theorists whose reliance upon single senses has misled them so badly.

If it was clear all the time to ordinary observation that the world was not like the one described by the philosophers, nobody raised any objections. In the nineteenth century they did, but because of certain connection, these later thinkers continued to miss the point. Schopenhauer, still hopelessly enmeshed in the Kantian orbit, talked about the 'will', by which he meant to describe and to generalize the kind of force which exists at the physical level, but that did not get him out of the charmed subjective circle.

Nietzsche was perhaps the first European philosopher of any moment to acknowledge the importance of force. Unlike Schopenhauer, however, he saw it exclusively in socio-cultural terms. What a different turn philosophy might have taken had either Schopenhauer or Nietzsche recognized the importance of artifacts, those material objects which are altered through human agency for human uses! But both men were victims of that subjective orientation which plagued philosophers and did not allow them to come to grips with the objective and independent nature of that material world in which artifacts play such an integral part. Culture for them was purely a personal affair, and they saw it as an element of society into which it had been projected by individuals.

The qualities, as the philosophers have traditionally understood them, are the familiar ones corresponding to the senses: they dealt with the senses of taste, smell, hearing, sight, the four so-called skin senses: touch, warmth, cold, and pain, in addition to the organic sensations, such as hunger and thirst. Finally, they knew about but did not deal with the muscle sense, which issues from nerve endings deep in the muscle fibers, and records the weight of objects, their hardness or softness, and, most important, their resistance. So preoccupied were the philosophers with the senses themselves that they forgot to notice what those senses reported. This is understandable when we remember that most philosophers tended toward epistemological idealism. The sense of resistance has not even yet received sufficient recognition as the sense which corresponds to the existence of forces. Force is a sense quality, resulting from the combination of skin touch and muscle tension. It records the existence of external events.

That it is not a quality but a primary quality is attested by the fact that we all have material bodies and exist in a world of other material bodies, with some of which we make contact. An individual who was blind, deaf, and dumb could still feel physical encounters with other bodies, would still have the sense of touch, and could still experience resistance.

Force, then, provides the entering wedge to the understanding of much in the nature of man and the world he inhabits. And force as a physical effect, as what changes or tends to change the state of rest or motion of a body, has not been neglected. What has been neglected, however, is the nature of force as a quality.

CHAPTER VI

LANGUAGE AS A MATERIAL TOOL

The aim of all organisms is survival. Man is no exception, but he has extended his aim quantitatively until it amounts to a qualitatively different affair, for he aims also at ultimate survival. Thus he has added the need to stay alive permanently to the more pressing need to stay alive immediately. These aims can be reached only by dealing with the environment, and he must dominate it sufficiently to be able to make over the materials in it into forms more suited to his needs. Human behavior may be defined as the active response of the individual to the stimulus from a material object. It consists in the interaction between man and material, with the man endeavoring to alter the material. Usually, language is involved in human activity in some way, for language is the form in which beliefs are stored, and men act largely from beliefs. Thus action depends to some extent upon the use of language, and we see in this aspect the functioning of language as a material tool.

Languages are, of course, not individual but social inventions. The individual must plan and cooperate with his fellows. The plans have to be stored and they have to be communicated. A communication does not become a language until it achieves symmetry by involving a two-way operation. Unless the sender of a message can exchange roles with the receiver on the occasion of the next message, it is not legitimate to call a mechanism of communication a language. Thus the chemical code of information in the genetic material of organisms which instructs the next generation how to make a duplicate of its parents is not a language, although it is a communication. Both symbolic communication systems and languages can be seen to be necessities of survival. The most familiar of such systems are the colloquial languages, the natural languages which have developed in the course of the life of communities.

Let me begin with a more primitive account. Survival is possible to the individual only by coming to terms with his immediate environment: meeting its demands (conditioning) and extracting from it what he needs. Both involve interactions. The stimuli to language-using are the material things in his immediate environment which threaten injury or extinction, or which suggest need-reductions. Continual encounters with these or like objects (members of the same class which can be readily identified as such) call for naming in order to facilitate recognition upon subsequent occasions.

Language arose as a response to these interactions. Recognizing objects again involves naming, and socially referring to them in order to deal with tasks too large for the individual requires the making of sentences (combining the names). Thus language, which consists of signs in the form of shaped sound waves and of scratches on hard surfaces, is a material tool invented in order to deal with other materials.

I have said that language is a material tool. And as we shall see later, it refers to material things. Thus both in itself and in its use, it is material. I say 'material' rather than 'physical' because the physical is the first level of organization of material. There are no non-physical materials since the integrative levels of organization are cumulative upward, but we call those materials which have merely the physical properties 'physical'. All organizations of matter above the physical, such as the chemical, the biological, the psychological, and the cultural, bear those names. Thus matter is a neutral term with respect to the organizations of it, but is always at least physical.

Language, then, we can now say is a material tool at the psychological and cultural levels. A language is a conventionally established signalling system. Language in use consists in chains of discretely coded signals which pass through material channels of transmission and are then decoded. The channels may be naturally occurring materials, such as air, or artificially contrived ones, such as telephone lines.

Wittgenstein, in his *Tractatus*, has described how he thought language could be constructed, and he certainly did describe how some of it was constructed. Material things are named, and the names combined in elementary propositions. The elementary propositions are then combined in complex propositions. The multiplication of complex propositions makes up a fine mesh network which mirrors the world. Thus language is called into existence to describe and to deal with material things. No doubt, such constructivism occurs, but there are other methods, for instance, induction to hypotheses which are then measured against relevant portions of the world, and deductions from axioms which are then applied to the world as a test of their representation. But all of this involves relations with materials which still constitute the criteria of truth or falsity. An ordinary language is an open system in almost every respect. Its syntax is continually undergoing revision, and its vocabulary continually being altered as words change their meanings or flow into or out of it.

Language fascinates philosophers because of its complex and elusive nature, and lately because it seems some place to go for men who have read themselves out of the scientific purview. But, as I hope to show, there is nothing mysterious about it, and indeed it may be considered that part of material culture in which communication blends with storage for purposes of control, a tool like any other, even though a pervasive and indispensible one, and so part of technology.

If we define an 'artifact' as a material altered through human agency to make it suitable for human uses, then there seem to be two kinds: signs and the reference of signs, or symbols and tools. In this sense, a building is a tool as much as a bulldozer, a violin as much as a paved street. This is quite conventional usage, but it may seem a bit more odd to say that a language is a particular kind of artifact or tool. But isn't it? A language is an artifact because it uses shaped materials, in this case, sound waves which have been altered in specific ways through human agency, or scratches on smooth surfaces. To this end clay has been used, and so have papyrus reeds, palm fronds, strips of bamboo, wood, stone, and leather. The symbols have been pictures, but more commonly they are abstract signs to which conventional meanings have been arbitrarily attached. By means of languages men refer to other material objects. A language is a set of signs together with the rules for combining them in order to make indicators of material objects or events. Often the language refers to expressions in other languages, but eventually there is a material reference for the second language reference, or for the third, or whatever. Eventually, all signs point to materials or their properties.

Language can be considered as a branch of the more general

classification of communication theory, where it joins communication engineering and information theory. In this way, the emphasis is put on language as technology and on the material media rather than on the messages which are sent. It will be necessary to say a word about each of them.

The material media have been vastly improved in the last few centuries. In addition to the written word on paper, we now have the recorded spoken word on plastic records which can be played back, we have the telephone, the wireless telegraph, we have computer programming on tape, the radio, and television. Many of these are two-way media, but some are one-way.

The information theoretic analysis of language has disclosed some interesting facts about it, and we might here sum them up. The individual is a source, his formulation in language of the message he wishes to send is his version of an encoding transmitter, and the person who hears him or who receives his writing is the decoding receiver. There are no messages without a medium, a material channel through which the message can be sent and which has been devised for that sole purpose. Some materials must be used: sound waves or scratches on paper. The construction of a message is a kind of communication engineering, and its use a kind of human engineering — what has been called "the engineering of consent."

The symbolic nature of language is hardly a topic that anyone could rightly describe as neglected. But the material nature of language could be so described. It has been considered negligible where it has been acknowledged at all. That the medium influences the message, however, is just beginning to be somewhat understood. Like most such sudden understandings, it tends to be overstated, as with McLuhan, who evidently considered that the medium *is* the message. The truth, however, lies somewhere south of that. It is well known that telegrams constrict language, and that the mechanical printing press elaborates it. But the skillful communicator makes words say what he wants them to say, and not what *they* want to say or what their medium *inclines* him to say.

No doubt, the media do influence the messages which are sent over them. A large part of this influence is what the communication engineers have called "noise": interference from the type of material used or the form of expression employed, in either case the degree to which the medium conditions the message. But there is another, and in many ways more serious, type of distortion, and it comes not from the medium but from the anticipated character of the decoding receiver. The rule for this is simple enough. As a result of observations made thus far, at least, it is fair to say that the more far-reaching the media, the more trivial the message. Radio and television have developed no Homers, no Shakespeares, no Bachs. Popular media are apt to drag down what comes over them to a level which is intelligible to those whose intellectual equipment is not very great. The same is true of most newspapers and popular magazines, and even books: the greater the circulation, the more superficial the contents. This is not an absolute rule, of course, but it is indicative of a strong statistical trend.

It can be insisted, however, that this development is the fault of those in charge of the media, or of the system whereby the media are financially supported. So long as commercial advertising firms or governments which rest on the support of the masses must furnish the funds, the appeal will be to the greatest number of people who can possibly be reached. More definitely, then it is the fault of the system. It must either be supplemented or replaced.

Some language recites how to deal with materials, how to alter them in ways which bring them into conformity with the reduction of human needs. Formulas, the equations of applied science and technology, textbooks, recipes, are clear instances. They are, in a certain sense, kinds of engineering directions.

The distinction between the natural and the artificial is curious and in many ways misleading. The artificial ought not to be opposed to the natural, but considered a special and if need be a peculiar part of it. Man is a natural animal, and what a natural animal makes is also natural. When he alters near-by bits of the available environment to further the reduction of his own needs, there is no good reason to think the result non-natural. It is artificial-natural, that part of the natural world which has been altered through human agency.

Now let us consider the ordinary or colloquial languages in this connection. They are collections of artifacts which are combined uneasily and loosely to make up an instrument of communication. There are all sorts of oddities about them. For instance, no one has ever used an entire language, only segments of it. It is to be doubted

whether in fact anyone ever knew or spoke an entire language. So the
individual is always in the strange condition of relying heavily upon
an instrument which consists in parts of which he must know some
only, and out of this knowledge select the small finite combinations he
wishes to use. There are more than half a million words in the English
language, but a sentence, which is the unit of expression, seldom
contains more than a few dozen. This is one peculiarity.

There is another. Other tools have always been the result of
deliberate effort. But in language, we have the spectacle of a tool which
grew up unplanned over the generations, continually being enlarged
and amended unofficially and unprofessionally. Street slang, which
may be the work of illiterates, may pass permanently into common
coin. For the fact is that anyone who speaks a language may influence
its subsequent use. There are no authorities in charge of this function;
it operates freely and clearly. That the *most* unplanned and uncontrolled
of human tools should also be the largest and most indispensable
presents a paradox.

The colloquial languages were not planned as wholes, but they have
properties as wholes nevertheless. It was noted by A.N. Whitehead
and others that philosophies are implicit in them, in their grammar
and vocabulary, but more especially in their syntax. A philosophy in
this sense is a system of total explanation, and it is so imbedded in the
language that to learn the language is to accept the explanation. But
such dominant implicit philosophies were not planned as such, not
constructed deliberately; they evolved as the language itself evolved,
until one day they made their presence felt as essential parts of everyday
communication. Speaking a language in any full sense of the phrase
means taking for granted in the hearer or reader the same set of
fundamental beliefs as exists in the speaker. Much more is encoded
and sent out over the channels, received and decoded, than either the
sender or the receiver knows as a matter of conscious awareness.
Whitehead complained that to express a new philosophy in an old
language, which already had its own philosophy, involved a conflict
and a confusion that threatened communication.

The point is that when we use an ordinary language, we include in
the use, without knowing that we do so, some extraordinary factors.
In principle, propositions should not be accepted by belief without
examination, and the more fundamental the beliefs, the more careful

the examination. For, as I have noted, we act from our beliefs, but the gravity of the situation is intensified when we remember that we act crucially and critically from our most fundamental beliefs. And so we should be extremely careful what we admit to the status of belief. In this direction ordinary language is beguiling, and slips over on us much of which we have not examined and would not have accepted.

The almost religious faith in the efficacy of ordinary language which possesses Austin and Ryle and their followers is a consequence of the Scottish school of common sense given a linguistic turn by G. E. Moore and Wittgenstein. It is logical to assume that ordinary language is the natural vehicle for the expression of common sense. The trouble with ordinary language is that it does not embody the entire breadth of human experience, as it once may have done. It does not embody the experience of the scientist in his laboratory with his instruments, a fantastically great range extending all the way from the test tube to the space craft. For these experiences, he needs the large number of technical languages he has invented for the purpose, and he needs the complexities of mathematics.

A peculiarity of technology is that, in engineering, we never know who will be served. A bridge builder cannot tell who will walk over his bridge, or how many or for how long. The Roman road builders in Britain did not envisage the modern traffic which passes over it. This is not a critical problem, and it does not have results which are critical, even though they are far-ranging. But with the use of language as a material tool, the situation is quite different. For in communication engineering, we have the unusual situation that the message is held in the channel indefinitely. We can still decode ancient Egyptian hieroglyphics and Assyrian cuneiform. It is relatively easy to be the cause of a series of effects, but absolutely impossible to predict with any accuracy what the effects will be, how widespread in space and time, or how forceful. The writer and recorder may be speaking to future generations many thousands of years removed and, as in the case of Greek philosophy, for instance, have an immense and unforeseen effect on cultures which at the time could not even have been envisaged.

Not only is language itself a material tool, but its use is also material. I take it that all language refers to material things, directly or indirectly. If directly, then by specifying what is true of a class; if indirectly, then by referring to other language which refers to material things directly.

Presence for any language-user being the limited thing it is, the reference of language is always more to absent than to present objects. If, for instance, I were to say that all men are mortal, I would be referring to the preponderance of absent men as much as to the tiny sample of men who are present.

Language is that technology in which we attempt to describe and to deal in a special way with the similarities we discover in material things. That is why language is so incurably general. A brief glance at the material theory of reference will serve as illustration.

Words are shaped sounds or inscriptions which are used as names, and of course, for all names there are things named. Every name is the name *of* something. Material things are named, and so are the parts of material things which are themselves material things. Thus the White House in Washington is a material thing, and so is its roof.

Words name four kinds of things: either material things or their parts, properties of material things, classes of material things, or classes of classes of material things, for there is nothing else to name. Examples are a house, a planet; round or blue; the class of all houses or of all planets; and furniture (the class of all classes of chairs, tables, etc.) or numbers.

Sentences connect names. When they do so, they form new names. When these can be either true or false (or indeterminate), we call them propositions. Propositions are of three kinds: they may be (a) singular material propositions, (b) universal material propositions, or (c) universal formal propositions.

A singular material proposition is one which refers to an individual material thing. A universal material proposition is one which refers to all material things of a given class throughout the cosmos. A universal formal proposition is one which refers *indirectly* to all material things, without restriction as to class, by referring *directly* to abstract things.

It is interesting that the elaborate technology of the material theory of reference, by means of which we can designate material things either individually or in general, was the outcome of the practical exigencies of dealing with the immediate environment in order to reduce the many organic needs.

Thus while the conveyance of language is always an affair of physical technology, it is different from the meaning. But the meaning, too, is material, as I have argued. Propositions may be true or false, but so long as their truth or falsity is unknown or they are known to be true, they are accepted by belief. No doubt, language influences action since we act from our beliefs, that is to say, on the basis of those propositions which are known or suspected to be true. But it is also the case that action influences language. We name what we encounter and then combine the names into sentences, and our encounters are increased through movement and activity. Because of the traditional interest in reason and sense perception, the role of the musculature and of all activities in the derivation of reliable knowledge has been vastly underplayed in knowledge theory.

Let us come at the technological problem from another perspective. Communication is social, and the construction of society does not consist merely in human individuals, but always in human individuals mediated by some material artifact. If we remember that ordinary languages are artificial constructions (in the sense that they consist in altered materials, and that they could have been constructed of the same materials altered in other ways), then it is true that any relation between two human individuals almost always is mediated by an artifact. Materials altered through human agency — artifacts — furnish the cement by means of which two human individuals are brought into contact and, in greater numbers, built into social institutions. Thus the more developed the technology, the more advanced the institution. Technology is the driving force of human culture as well as the means by which culture is made possible at all.

Rarely is a language used without other tools, and even more rarely are other tools used without language. The speculations carried on in science and technology deal with the similarities we suspect to exist in material things. Our discoveries and inventions in the design and control of some of the potentialities of materials are conducted in terms of a language of some sort. Thus language as a tool is usually related to other kinds of tools.

Great delicacy is required to be sure that the instrument by means of which communication is undertaken remains chiefly a means and does not interfere overly much with the message. There is, of course, always some "noise." Theoretically, the meaning of a sentence is the same, whether it is spoken or written, if the same expressions in the same language are used, but a little experience with adapting one form of literature to another will convince even the most radical sceptic that this is not the case. The translation from play to novel or from novel to play is more often than not unsuccessful. We ought therefore to talk not merely about languages — they do not occur in isolation but always in material media — but about the material media themselves, in a word about the relation between meaning and the mechanisms of communication.

In considerations of meaning, denotation must be sharply distinguished from connotation. In direct communication, say a statistical report, denotation is uppermost and connotation minimal, if it exists at all. In indirect communication, say a short story, connotation is uppermost and denotation minimal. Let us confine our attention now to the direct communication. Here, the uncertainty of the meaning of a sentence is decreased with the increase in the number of times it is used in communication. If the sentence is widely applicable, it will be used frequently in connection with different kinds of occasions, and so it will acquire a number of connotations which increase the uncertainty of its denotation. For the greater the number of possible meanings, the greater the degree of randomness, and the number of possible meanings decreases the probability of successful decoding. Thus the entropy of the meaning of a sentence is a function of the frequency of its use.

In this way, technology enters into the question of meaning. Since the meanings of material things change, the language changes with them and there are no fixed meanings; what was decoded might differ from what was encoded. The mace was once a weapon of war, then it became a symbol of sovereignty, next a staff of office borne before designated officials, and now it is an expression of status. The designation of a message will be altered in ways not indicated from the source. *Communication is more damaging when it is thought to exist and does not than when it is thought not to and does.*

In his second book, the *Investigations*, Wittgenstein turned against language and charged it with obscuring our view of the material world. He proposed that a close analysis of ordinary language would reveal the degree of distortion, a knowledge which we would need in order to dispel it and thus come to an unimpeded set of perceptions. But in all this there is assumed the correspondence theory of truth: that when language correctly represents the material world, then and only then is matter allowed to speak for itself.

The problem, then, for more precise communication is to build a communication system in which the meanings can be standardized by constructing channels which do not allow appreciable alterations in the message. This might require a direct attack on the rigidities of language. The more subtle the ideas to be communicated, the more flexible the language require. The deliberate modifications of ordinary language have seldom, if ever, been undertaken, but they are not beyond the bounds of possibility. It is only necessary to consider that technological aspects of language do exist, and to regard language itself, together with everything that it conveys, as properties of that most complex of all things which we have come to call matter.

CHAPTER VII

CULTURE AS CONCRETE ONTOLOGY

My thesis in this chapter concerns the nature of culture understood to be the same as concrete — as contrasted with abstract — ontology. I am, of course, aware that this is not the conventional conception of either culture or ontology, but I propose to offer here a certain theory concerning the relations of that part of philosophy named 'ontology' to those large-scale items in the social field known as 'human cultures', more specifically, in the use of ontologies as instruments of cultural analysis. Therefore, to make it clear I shall have to explain (I) what I mean by culture, (II) what I mean by ontology, (III) how ontology functions as culture, (IV) how culture functions as ontology, and (V) ending with some general remarks.

I

The smallest human isolate is a culture, not an individual. The test for valid isolation is the prospect of separate survival: the individual cannot live alone, a culture can. I define culture as what is contained in the works of man and their effects (including their effects on man); more specifically, as collections of individuals, social groups, and institutions, together with their tools and their languages, organized around a central doctrine which may be either expressed or unexpressed but is assumed implicitly by all of its components through their very participation. A culture, in this sense, may be described as the common use of a set of complex ideas by the members of a social group employing tools, folkways, and institutions over a broad area whose boundaries are recognized.

Collectively, culture is a material construction erected upon the effort to supply all of the basic human requirements. All individuals are members of the same animal species and all have the same set of needs, primarily those for water, food, and sex, and secondarily, for information, activity, and security. It is always difficult for any investigator to believe that fundamentally he is dealing with the same biological man when he encounters the outward aspects of widely diverse cultures, the culture of a West European, say, that of a native in the interior of New Guinea, a cultivated Chinese from Hong Kong, and a South African bushman. There is ample room within the range of cultures for them to swing widely in many different directions.

Institutions constitute the first organizational level in the analysis of cultures. An institution is itself an organization, and consists of an established group of human individuals together with their customs, laws, and material artifacts, all held together by a central aim or purpose. I define artifacts as materials which have been altered through human agency to make them suitable for human uses; everything, in fact, from skyscrapers to skillets. Those who inhabit advanced cultures live almost entirely in an artificial or "built" environment, one consisting of a variety of artifacts. There is almost nothing in a civilized individual's surroundings that was not constructed for the purpose, including even the ground he walks on and the air he breathes.

Of course, languages are among the most important artifacts; they are artifacts because they are carried by signs made by marks on hard surfaces or by sound waves shaped to convey meanings. Languages are, in fact, indispensable parts of the cultures they serve and in which they are securely imbedded. The key to their understanding must consist, finally, in the roles they perform in the culture as enabling invariants.

Individuals are parts of a culture because they have acquired the abilities to cope with it. These include the skills necessary to deal with artifacts, the cultivated sensibilities resulting from that experience, and the knowledge to oversee the whole enterprise. The effects of culture upon the individual are in a way overwhelming. Culture is such a pervasive affair, however, that many remain unaware of its existence. They simply assume that this is just the way things are. The cultural background of ideas, habit patterns, and feelings contains such immense similarities that it is hardly noticeable.

Most individuals, like most institutions, are culture-bound. That is to say, they accept a system of ideas, move among a set of artifacts, and have their own preferred way of feeling and doing things, that together constitute the culture. Cultures may overlap or they may be mutually incompatible, but there is no possibility of an empty culture space between them; and so the only way two cultures may be compared, contrasted, or evaluated is from the perspective provided by a third, in which, presumably, the same limitations would prevail.

However, all cultures are in one sense limited affairs and in another sense unlimited. Since they depend upon living men and material orgainzations of artifacts and languages, they manifest the same life-cycle as do all other material organizations: they come into existence, develop, reach a peak, decline, and disappear, and in that sense they are limited. But at the same time, their life-cycle is conducted all on their own momentum and never under the control of any human agency. Everyone contributes to them, but no one understands them altogether. In that sense, they may be said to be unlimited.

II

So much for the understanding of cultures. Before I can relate them to ontology, my next task must be to explain what I mean by ontology. Here we are on familiar ground, and I will not dwell on it. I employ the term, ontology, simply as a synonym for metaphysics, with the following distinction: metaphysics is speculative, while ontology is systematic. Metaphysics examines the question of what there is; ontology presents the conclusions in orderly form. Ontology, then, is the widest of any finite set of systems. It would, perforce, have to be an abstract body of knowledge and make the claim to truth, and this could be either a tentative or an absolute claim. Its own terms of description are those of the classic categories of traditional metaphysics, such as 'form', 'matter', 'reality', 'appearance', etc. The definition advanced by Bentham, that ontology is "the field of supremely abstract entities", will do nicely, for it refers to those categories, or, as we should say in modern logic, to the undefined terms employed in the unproved propositions which constitute the axioms of the system.

There is no official ontology, and contending ontologies must support their claims on the basis of the same criteria used by other kinds of systems: consistency, comprehensiveness, and applicability. They exist as theory in the written and spoken words of the professional philosophers. We shall see that their practical effects are somewhat more concrete, for they exist also — and more dynamically — as the actual ingredients of cultures.

III

When we isolate the philosophy of a culture, we are, so to speak, penetrating to its essence logically considered (its essence axiologically considered cannot be analyzed structurally but can only be felt). A philosophy is what a culture means; only in the past, we have had too narrow a conception of philosophy. Classical philosophies are suspect as inadequate simply on the face value of their simplicity. Abstract systems of philosophy could be promulgated which would be far more complex than any we have before us now. We shall have to reach such a degree of complexity if we are to comprehend the kind of philosophy underlying the vast cultures we call civilizations. The probabilities are that the kind of philosophy requisite for the kind of culture we encounter currently has not yet been envisaged by the philosophers.

In practice, ontologies may be recognized as bundles of complex propositions. The propositions, however, must be understood as objective because they are extracted from the external material world and are referred back to it. Another name for such a bundle is the 'implicit dominant ontology'. It is ontological because it refers to ultimate problems of being, it is dominant because it takes precedence over all the thought, feelings, and actions of the members of the social group which holds it to be true, and it is implicit because it is unconsciously believed and followed. I call the ontology of a culture its 'implicit dominant ontology' because it is assumed and often unknown, and because in this guise it tends to control everything else.

Every culture has its own implicit dominant ontology and is permeated by it, but since the environmenting conditions for every culture differ, each finds itself in a special climate, terrain, and neighborhood. Thus a culture, we may now say in a revised definition, is the actual selection of some part of the whole arc of possible human behavior considered in its effects upon materials, such as artifacts and social institutions, made according to the demands of some specific implicit dominant ontology, and modified by the total environment.

Nothing less than a systematic metaphysics — an ontology — could function as a set of axioms so broad that every aspect of culture assumes it. Ontologies furnishes the consistency of cultures. A culture is a kind of concrete system, but what is a system if not a consistency of elements? Now when a system is so large that we call it a culture, its consistency has to rest on some very wide base, on something as broad, in fact, as an ontology. On what other base could one rest the compatibility which is found between the individual members of a society, or between the social groups and their artifacts, or between both and the institutions in which they are engaged?

Implicit dominant ontologies become social philososophies when they are adopted by societies as the result of some kind of shock — a social revolution, say, or a defeat in war. Christianity could never have triumphed to the extent that it did without the destruction of Rome by the Goths. The Roman ethos rested on the physical force of military power, and when this was dissipated by a counter-force, it left a vacuum, together with the assumed stipulation that the new power would have to take some other form. And when the transition occurred from the Middle Ages to the Renaissance in Europe, the social revolution brought with it a new set of assumptions which can be traced through the Reformation, through the discovery of experimental science, through the growth of industrialism, through the rebirth of classical learning, through the rise of the cities, through the development of democracy.

Ontologies in this sense, then, are empirical affairs since they are all-pervasive in cultures and are to be found in any and every part. The implicit dominant ontology (or i.d.o. as we may call it now for brevity) is a concrete ontology but also a transparent one, for it lies deeply imbedded in cultures and reaches into every corner of them, yet the bare bones do not protrude. A certain amount of searching is necessary in order to detect its presence. It comes closest to the surface and may be discerned best in six places: (i) in the rational social unconsciousness of the human individual, (ii) in the hierarchial arrangement of institutions, (iii) in the myth of the leading institution, (iv) in customs, (v) in the kind of fine arts which are prevalent, and finally, (vi) in questions of taste as exhibited in the adopted set of preferences. A few words now about each of these.

(i) The first place in which the i.d.o. can be detected coming closest to the surface is what may be called the rational social unconsciousness. In the individual, it consists of those beliefs which he holds in common with the other members of his society without, in the least, knowing that he holds them. They constitute the basis of his sanity and are maintained implicitly. They seldom rise to consciousness, but whatever does so is often a direct logical consequence of them. When confronted with them, the individual is likely to express surprise that anyone would ever question their truth, as though they were held by all members of all societies when, in fact they are not. A good test to determine whether a belief belongs in the rational social unconsciousness is to suggest its opposite or contradictory. If this is considered "inconceivable," it is clear evidence of the presence of a fundamental belief.

For example, in such terms, the majority of the members of the western cultures or Europe and the Americas are materialists, meaning by this some variety of non-Marxist materialism. Though many would profess a species of idealism, their actions are in definite disagreement. Most professional philosophers are subjective idealists rather than materialists, thus revealing a sharp cleavage between the philosophy professionally held and the one widely practiced. Few among us really believe — and none act — as though our knowings make a difference to the things that we know.

(ii) The second place where the i.d.o. comes closest to the surface of the culture is in the hierarchy of social institutions. Most cultures are composed of the same set of institutions, even though these may have been developed to quite different degrees and may be quite distinct in character. What distinguishes cultures is the order of importance in which their institutions have been arranged. In medieval Europe, for instance, the Church came right after the state at the top of the order; while in the United States today that position is given to applied science.

(iii) The third place where the i.d.o. manifests itself is in the myth of the leading institution. I employ the term 'myth' here as a belief carrying the most important values, not as a false theory. Truth or falsity here is irrelevant to the purpose of a belief and its effects in practice. The myth is the set of beliefs emotionally accepted and promoted by the leading institution. It is the truth as accepted and symbolically presented, as the independent counterpart of the ethos, the result of the efforts of the ethos to get itself objectified and externalized by the members of the social group of the culture.

Good examples can always be found in absolute and official beliefs, such as the holy trinity of Christianity: the Father, the Son, and the Holy Ghost; and the correspondingly established trinity of Marxism: Marx, Engels, and Lenin, in what Toynbee called in a telling phrase, "the holy atheistic church militant."

(iv) The fourth place where the i.d.o. is to be seen is in established customs which have been sanctified by long practice. They are clearly visible in the oldest of still-existing cultures, the Indian and the Chinese. A good example was the practice of suttee in India, the voluntary acton on the part of a Hindu widow of the upper classes who joined the body of her god-husband on the funderal pyre as a way of rejoining him after death by means of the purifying flames, a custom so strong that the British in 1793 decided to abandon their efforts to abolish it. In China, the belief that ancestors were divinities led to their worship as early as the Shang Dynasty (1766-1122 B.C.). When courtiers sent to the eldest son of Shih Huang Ti a forged letter purporting to come from his father, the Emperor, and ordering him to commit suicide, he obeyed immediately (210 B.C.). Both Indian and Chinese cultures survived because of a supreme emphasis on the institution of the family with its ritual and implied ethical standards, and behind these, the presence of ontologies can be clearly discerned.

(v) The fifth place in which the i.d.o. comes close to the surface is in the fine arts which the culture develops as peculiarly its own. Art does not have to do with didactic beliefs, of course, but rather with qualities and values (which are, after all, nothing more or less than high qualities), with the symbolic expression of fundamental beliefs. There is no reason to suppose that beliefs do not show here also, no less so for having been arrived at in an indirect fashion and with different means of expression. The arts cut deeply, and what rises by their means to the world available to awareness has welled up from profoundly immersed forces which are strongly influential in the culture.

It would be difficult to divorce the method of Cézanne, for example, when he insisted that what he was trying to paint were "sensations in the presence of nature," from the empiricism of the experimental scientists of his day, who were endeavoring to accomplish the same ends in a more rational and even a mathematical language. Again, the subjective ontologies of India are made evident in their tension dances in which the attainment of bodily control counts for as much as it does in the religious practices of Yoga.

(vi) The sixth place in which the i.d.o. of a culture comes closest to the surface is in the set of preferences which the individuals in a given culture exhibit. The examination of any popular set will reveal the ontology at work. These signs are not infallible, but they serve as rough guide-posts where otherwise we have none. It takes some time for the ontology of a culture to make its way upward to that superficial place occupied by matters of taste, but this is in some fashion the surest, even though it be the last, manifestation. If two friends pass up an invitation to the formal opening of an art gallery in order to attend a professional football game, they are exhibiting the common possession of a set of preferences. But in doing this, they are doing much more. For the preference they show by sharing hooks up through consistency with other such preferences which they hold in common with many people. And so we come to the discovery of the foundations of that consistency which is society-wide, and we find in the end that it represents nothing less than an ontology.

IV

Thus far I have been presenting the relations between ontology and culture from the perspective afforded by culture. In other words, I have been considering the cultural functions of ontology. We can turn the picture around now and briefly view the relations between ontology and culture from the perspective afforded by ontology by considering the ontological functions of culture. Where culture has been our chief concern, ontology will be substituted.

The fundamental theory of ontology involves inquiries which can in a certain sense never be answered with any finality or absoluteness. Yet actual cultures are themselves the frozen answers to ontological problems. Unless such answers are made tentatively, they tend to block further inquiry. This is the sense in which philosophy can act as a liberating force, as Russell pointed out. It sets us free of abstractions which we have been accepting through implicit beliefs. But the force of tradition, which is the conditioned habits of cultures, is against change of any kind. In short, cultures inhibit further investigations by giving final answers to ultimate questions.

Most human cultures, then, are accompanied by inhibited inquiry. Although themselves the results of inquiry, one of their by-products is that they stand in the way of further inquiry. If curiosity is almost as basic as food and sex, frustrated inquiry may be almost as disastrous to society as frustrated sexual desires are to the individual. The difficulties of some societies may be the direct outcome of blocked inquiry. For the fact is that individuals and human cultures do not live on the unsolved problems of philosophy but rather on incorporated and institutionalized solutions. Life, both individual and social, is impossible otherwise, or so it appears; and therefore it is the purpose of what Emerson labeled "perpetual inquiry" to insure that such acceptance is never irrevocable. For an individual or an entire culture can progress only to the extent to which change is allowable; and genuine improvement is possible only when the final truth is held to be unknown, and, even better, unknowable. Militant faith in stock solutions may be traditional practice, but it is also bad philosophy. We do not have a firm tradition based on the acceptance of the postulate of an unaffiliated truth or of a detached and disinterested search, but we had better develop one before it is too late.

The speculative ontological problem may now be reformulated somewhat as follows. Given the actual concrete ontologies as empirical elements of analysis, obtained by the above method, they set up a comparative study for the purpose of seeking a better theoretical ontology, where by 'better' here is meant one which is more consistent and more comprehensive than any to date, and would therefore be capable of producing a fuller culture. The better ontology will not result from a mere choice among the existing alternatives, but will rather be an imaginative construct suggested by them, embracing what they have to offer of value and truth, but eliminating their shortcomings. The history of philosophy is the chronological recital of a succession of theoretical ontologies whose practical role does not seem to have been well understood. All we have been offered are social interpretations of the effects of the times upon the philosophers; we are not given the dynamic interactions of the societies and the philosophies. Theoretical ontology has a concrete existence which does not make it any less theoretical. There is nothing more practical than the use of abstract theory, as relativity physics and quantum mechanics have demonstrated. The great philosopher is potentially a culture-maker in the grand sense, but he must work with the materials and depend upon the findings of the empirical ontologist. In this sense, too, the cultural anthropologist and the sociologist are field workers in ontology; and philosophy, to the extent to which it is held down to actual human cultures, is nothing more or less than social science.

The aim of the theory set forth here has been to further the claims of the search for truth, but I have been occupied chiefly with methodology in an attempt to save philosophy from vagueness by pointing out the ready made existence of empirical ontologies which cab be studied in the field. To bring the speculative and empirical branches of ontology together after the manner of scientific empiricism means to discover for ontology a way in which it can be used for the prediction and control of actual cultures.

V

The foregoing discussion of culture, ontology, and their interrelations suggests a few tentative conclusions. Certainly the classic conceptions of philosophy, however useful, are inadequate, for philosophy can no longer be confined to the abstract speculations of the philosophers. We are theoreticians, but the theories we discuss can sometimes be discovered imbedded in cultures. What is new about this is that it represents research and development at the empirical level. We simply have not been thinking enough along lines which would make of the subject matter of the anthropologist and the historian fertile fields of data for the hypotheses of the observational ontologist. Therefore, I will need to say a few words about the empirical ontological problem and its approaches.

The organization of things and events *qua* organization is evidence of the force of ontology in actual practice. An organization is effective in proportion to the strength of its ontological axioms. To act inconsistently is to act illogically; to act astructurally is to act unmathematically; and to act against the axioms is to act anti-ontologically.

The empirical ontological problem, then, can be formulated as follows: given the institutions, tools, and folkways of actual cultures, to find the ontologies which underlie them. This involves investigation into the details of an actual cultural situation, an assignment both easier and more difficult than it sounds. Cultures are all of a piece and will give the same ring when struck in any vital spot. But on the other hand, considerable equipment on the part of the investigator is presupposed: a knowledge of the varieties of cultures and of types of ontologies. The task requires painstaking inquiry into, for instance, the graded meanings of the leading institution and its myth. It relies upon the use of the projective techniques furnished by empirical psychology, to interpret the implicit dominant ontology in the sub-consciousness of the individual. For the ontology there reveals itself indirectly, never directly. The investigator has to back up, so to speak, from the encounter with the details of actual conditions. For the theorist, in a given state, tribe, or country, it means to reconstruct the ontology which might have given rise to such conditions. He will have to subtract the environmental factors, which are brute and irreducible, constituting the framework within which the choice and application of beliefs was made; and he will have to devise an ontology on the basis of the solid remainder. Of course, this mechanism must not be understood as operating too consciously. Cultures were not developed by logicians armed with postulate-sets, and they must not be interpreted dogmatically simply because they can be analyzed in that way.

CHAPTER VIII

THE SPOKEN WORD

There are two missing chapters in the history of western philosophy, chapters containing names not to be found in the older standard histories. Ueberweg did not mention them, and neither did Erdmann or Windelband. I have looked also in many of the more recent histories, but without substantial results. Yet they were the names of men who were in their day exceedingly influential. The first of these was Isocrates, the second was a group of later sophists. They had in common that their field of endeavor was rhetoric, but they conceived it as a branch of philosophy: they were philosophers.

I

Isocrates was an orator whose work lay largely in the area of political philosophy. Perhaps the greatest educator of antiquity, he made a large fortune by teaching, lived to be 97, and was engaged in writing to the very end. He was frequently cited by Aristotle in his *Rhetoric*, and, according to Cicero, also emulated by Aristotle when he put his whole system into more polished form.[1] Although a well-known contemporary and friend of Plato, who called him in the Phaedrus a "companion" of Socrates and a genius, and praised him in the highest terms,[2] he was generally considered of lesser importance. And so he was when looked at from the point of view of the development of technical philosophy, but his work had a tremendous influence.

He has been credited with deliberately making rhetoric into an educational ideal as the preferred instrument of civic responsibility, and he gave to culture both an oratorical and a literary turn, in this way fostering the classical heritage that was passed on to Rome and the western educational tradition. One of his two broadest and most

enduring accomplishments, however, was the recognition of Hellenism
as the culture the Greek city-states had in common. Raising it almost
to the status of a religion, he called for a crusade on its behalf in an
effort to preserve and spread it. All of the evidence is contained in his
speeches, which are still available in three volumes in the Loeb Classical
Library.

He certainly presents a most curious figure: an orator who could
not himself speak in public because of a weak voice and nervousness,
and who therefore wrote down his speeches as a literary art form.
They were carefully composed and obviously intended to be a
possession forever. One of them which is still extant, the one addressed
to Philip, King of Macedon, had an almost immeasurable influence.
In it he urged King Philip to do for the Greek city-states what they
could not do for themselves: unite and invade Persia, which had overrun
Greece and been repulsed, but only with tremendous losses to the
Greeks. It continued to be a threat to them.

Before Philip could undertake this mission, he was assassinated, but
his son, Alexander who was only twenty-one at the time, took his place,
and in fact did far more than Isocrates had hoped, for he succeeded
in uniting the Greeks, and then with their troops and his own in the
next ten years conquered the whole eastern end of the Mediterranean,
including Egypt, and went on to take all of Asia as far out as the
westernmost provinces of India. When he died at the age of thirty-
two, his empire was divided among his generals, who continued to
promote everything Greek.

Thus the net effect of Isocrates' advice to Philip was to insure that
Greek civilization would be spread so widely that it was able to endure.
If we are now in a position to avail ourselves of its benefits, that is
probably due to the plan that Isocrates formulated. He may have been
the first ever to recognize that culture cuts deeper than race, for he
wanted to bestow the title of Hellenes "on those who share our culture
rather than those who share a common blood."[3]

Greece, in his day, was only a loose collection of independent city-
states which were more often than not engaged in internecine warfare.
At the time of the greatest Greek achievements, from the fifth to the
fourth centuries B.C., the people acknowledged only two institutions
in common: the Delphic Oracle and the Olympic Games. Now, thanks
to Alexander's efforts a hundred years later, the small Greek *polis* that

Plato advocated so strongly was replaced by the *cosmopolis*, in which form it had a better chance to survive.

We need to recall that in Isocrates' lifetime, speech could reach more people than writing. Indeed, it was reported that Demosthenes, when quite young, attended the lectures of Plato, but when he saw the crowds hastening to hear an oration by Callistratus, he deserted Plato and became a follower of Callistratus.[4] As Isocrates himself declared, there was no institution devised by man which the power of speech had not helped to establish. It was true. It would not be true today, for we are more inclined to estalish institutions by means of written documents. Writing then, remember, had to be composed by hand and reproduced in the same way, a slow and painful process, so that there were not at any given time too many copies circulating. It is quite remarkable, therefore, that any have survived; but of course, few have: we possess only a fraction of Greek literature and philosophy. The remainder perished long ago.

II

With the invention of printing, the whole situation changed radically. The balance tilted away from speech to writing; but this did not happen until some two thousand years later, and in the meanwhile there was another, and much more extensive, example of the power of oratory in philosophy.

Everyone, of course, is familiar with the achievements of Greek philosophy in the fifth century B.C. when Plato, Aristotle, and others were at work; but few have ever heard of a much later Greek renaissance in philosophy, and for a good reason: its leading advocates did not commit their ideas to writing but delivered them in public speeches, and so had an enormous contemporary influence, yet left nothing.

To make this account clearer, I will have to take something of a detour through the history of western philosophy, and, in the course of it, pay special attention to the little known part played by the early sophists.

The dialogues of Plato have had such a tremendous impact that his description of the sophists has been the prevailing one. Plato wrote, they did not; and so we have only his *Dialogues* to provide us with a knowledge of their teachings. I need not add that his was a highly prejudiced account, and there have been recent efforts to rehabilitate them. Plato had a great scorn for anything practical, and because they taught their pupils how to succeed in the world, he looked on them with contempt, but they were rewarded with high fees and great social esteem.

This is not to detract from Plato's main teachings; it means only that he was right in what he affirmed and wrong in what he denied. He discovered the domain of universals which was of great and permanent importance, indeed more so since the great prestige of pure mathematics and the laws of physics. But he refused to give the material world its due, and, as we know now, that world consists in far more than mere appearance. Without disparaging in the slightest the importance of his positive contribution, it is possible to say that there was more to the sophists of his day than he was willing to admit.

Plato characterized the sophists as skilled in disputation[5] and interested in winning arguments[6] rather than in pursuing the truth,[7] but they were also concerned with how language could be used for practical ends, and so practiced oratory and rhetoric. They were, at the time, the most successful teachers, well paid for their work and occupying an eminent position in society. Someone, after all, had to fill in a gap left by Plato, who had developed no theory for getting from theory to practice, no proposal for how to apply his metaphysics to the problems confronting a man who has to earn a living. Perhaps this was because he did not think well of practice; and if the sophists taught form rather than substance, it means that they left only a tradition of public speaking and a reputation for helping the sons of the fortunate.

But that is not the end of the story, though that is what we have been taught to believe. There have been two distinct historical periods of sophistic prominence, only the first of which is well known. The sophists of the period we have been talking about were those with whom Plato did battle. Their names are familiar enough: Gorgias, Hippias, Protagoras, among others. There is, however, another and most neglected chapter in the history of philosophy, one which describes a much later flourishing of sophists. Their time was the period when Hellenism was at its most influential, roughly in the first two Christian centuries.[8] There were at the time a number of centers of learning, and we know something of their importance. Athens was one, of course, and so also was Rome itself, but perhaps a few others can be mentioned, for they clustered around the edge of the Hellenic world: Pergamum, Antioch, the island of Rhodes, and Alexandria in Egypt. Philosophers often journeyed from one to another, and their fame in this way spread throughout the Empire, for the Romans accorded first place to Greek culture and felt so secure politically that the philosophers were free to express themselves, as free as they are today in western Europe and America. It took the Romans three hundred years to achieve this, for the Romans had conquered and annexed all of Greece, burned Corinth in 146 B.C., and carried off as slaves to Rome a thousand of the most cultivated Athenians. By 150 A.D. their descendents, the Greek philosophers, were among the wealthiest and most prestigious of citizens.

I have already mentioned some of the philosophers of the "second sophistic" in the last chapter — the name was coined by Philostratus,[9] who was one of them. They were concerned with form rather than substance; they put practical success before truth, and taught oratory rather than metaphysics. Skill in extempore declamations was particularly admired, for it was not *what* was said, so much as *how* it was said that counted. They wrote nothing, but the spoken word, even though no record of it was kept, was considered as significant as the written word; and therefore, rhetoric was held to be as important as philosophy. They did not advance knowledge, but they did help to found education as a formal discipline.[10] Theirs were the ideals of the spoken word: formal discourse, forensic argument, ritualized declamation. In this they followed their predecessors, but there were certain changes, and there was one sharp difference in particular: unlike their predecessors, they were classic Atticists who revered Plato and his dialogues.

It is a curious fact that the period when philosophers were the most highly regarded was the one in which they made the smallest contribution to their subject matter. They were eminent men who enjoyed the greatest social success ever accorded to a group of thinkers: next to the actual rulers of the time, they were the most powerful figures in society. They were treated like gods, were sent on important embassies, were helped to accumulate large fortunes, founded cities, and even had their marriages dynastically arranged. They were the popular heroes whose lectures attracted large crowds from all over the oikoumenê, the Greek diasporá, and were honored by having as their satirist Lucian (A.D. 120–180), the most famous literary man of the day.[11]

Cities competed for the privilege of harboring them and even of giving them burial. They were the darlings of the crowds, held important official position — and paradoxically were the ruin of philosophy, for the made surprisingly little or no contribution to general knowledge. Their work was notable for its almost total absence of content. Instead, there was a complete dedication to the practice of public speaking, a considerable attention to linguistic style and ornamentation, and the lowest record ever of solid achievement. It was a period of almost feverish activity, which left almost no trace.

The philosophers of the second sophistic were the ideal scholars, for they emulated everything that had been accomplished by the fifth and fourth century Greeks at Athens. Their lectures were subject to complex rules, which we do not know, but which their audiences. recognized,[12] and their language was confined to classical models. They utilized Isocrates' doctrine of Hellenism, and practiced it to impress on their Roman masters the inferiority of Roman culture. Dio Chrysostom compared them with lecherous eunuchs because nothing came of their desires for accomplishment, and they were quickly forgotten. So was their lesson that oratory is capable of wielding an immense social power; but, as we shall presently note, it may have to be revived.

III

The almost total conquest of printing over public speaking as a primary way of communicating, ever since Johannes Gutenberg invented the press in the fifteenth century of our era, can hardly be overestimated. We are now witnessing such a flood of printed material that we are unaware how much of it is waste and what work of quality goes unnoticed, yet it continues to be of tremendous influence. Recently, another revolutionary invention has quietly occurred, one which promises to be of equal importance: the television set. In conjunction with the other devices of telecommunications, the prospect is almost unlimited.

I don't think many of us have come yet to recognize what the effects of television could be. Eventually it may replace most printing. Think of it just in terms of the speed and reach of information. It is possible now for a public speaker, on short notice, to address everyone in the United States and indeed, nearly everyone in the entire western world, as happens, for instance, when a president of the United States avails himself of the advantage of a nation-wide hookup. In this way he can communicate with more people than he could by using all of the newspapers put together, and do so much faster.

Thus public speaking has returned, after an absence of centuries, as the more efficient way of utilizing language, and has reassumed an importance it has not had since Hellenistic times. The art of rhetoric, which is the discipline involved, must once more feature oratory as it did so long before the invention of printing. What happened to Marshall McLuhan is a sort of brief, but amazing illustration of what could happen again, and next time more widely. It is not many years since McLuhan with his doctrine that "the medium (of communication) is the message" was being paid $10,000 a lecture, a reminder of a practice that was quite common among the philosophers of the second sophistic.

Now McLuhan is dead and, what is worse, almost forgotten, as forgotten as those other philosophers who so long ago relied entirely on public speaking. Yet the experience could well be repeated by others, for we have a new instrument by which to inform ourselves, one which offers an immense advantage over the old. You don't even have to be literate to become part of the audience now, and you can make the acquaintance of the personality of the speaker, as well as hear his words, because you can watch him, as well as listen to him, while he is speaking.

The philosophers of the second sophistic left little by which we can remember them: little, that is, except the memory of an amazing success, more of a success, in fact, than philosophers have ever had either before them or since their day. This kind of oblivion is unlikely to occur again, because now every appearance of a speaker on television is preserved on videotape and thus made available to future generations.

It is much too early to say how and when this new tool will be used to its best advantage. Philosophers currently do not have much access to it because there is no great demand for their services, but this could change. The importance of philosophy is no less now than it ever was; only the recognition of it is. Television is capable of reviving the art of oratory far beyond the point to which it was carried for the ancient Romans by Cicero and others. It is just being admitted tentatively to some of our law courts.

We must remember, though, that the first use of any new technology is always a misuse. The airplane was first employed in war before being placed in the service of peacetime transportation. Nuclear fission was first developed to make atomic bombs and only later widely utilized as a source of energy to serve the general population. You are probably seeing television at its very worst right now, at least we can only hope so.

It may be, in short, that the dominance of the printed word is nearing an end, and that, thanks to television, the spoken word will resume its first place in the technology of communication. Surely we will be using it to teach philosophy, and so reaching more of an audience than we have been accustomed to lately. The personality of the teacher as well as the contents of his teachings are capable of weighing heavily, as they once did in ancient Athens and did again in the Greek centers of learning throughout the Roman Empire in the first two Christian centuries. And we will have a first impression, as well as a permanent record, of what the philosophers had to say, as well as how well they said it. And perhaps philosophy in this new guise will become recognized for the important topic that it is, which has not been true of it since the rise of the physical sciences.

CHAPTER IX

THE AMBIVALENCE OF AGGRESSION

The thesis I wish to argue here is that the ambivalent nature of aggression in the human, with its necessary destructive as well as constructive side, constitutes the chief obstacle confronting any program for the moralization of man. If we could account for this ambivalence, perhaps we might put ourselves in a position to rechannel the destructiveness and hence to solve the problem of morality more successfully than heretofore.

I

In the twenty-seven years since Dollard and his colleagues wrote about frustration and aggression, the evidence for the strength and primacy of aggression has accumulated steadily. They held it always to be the result of frustration,[1] and defined it independently as "an act whose goal response is injury to an organism,"[2] a view which has recently been supported by Buss,[3] for whom aggression is "an instrumental response that administers punishment," or "one that delivers noxious stimuli to another organism."

For me, aggression must be understood somewhat more broadly, and accordingly, I shall define it in terms of a drive to dominate the environment. More specifically, aggression is the alteration by an individual of a material object in the external world in order to effect a need reduction. Particular acts of aggression are usually prompted by some organ-specific need, such as food for the stomach, sex for the gonads, or knowledge for the brain.

In two thoughtful studies[4,5] which have appeared, the great European animal psychologists (or ethologists, as they like to call themselves) have argued that most animals are normally peaceful and only fight to protect a territory, to defeat a rival for a mate, or when threatened; and further, that such behavior is more a matter of predation than aggression; and that, even so, fighting is ritual and consists chiefly in posturing. Predation apart, when the weaker animal recognizes defeat, he throws himself upon his back and exposes his weakest spot, his belly, to lethal attack. But the victor does not take advantage of this opportunity; instead, he walks away, content to have established his supremacy. In captivity, all the rules are changed; but in the wild environment, animals (with some exceptions) do not engage in fighting to the death with other members of their own species, but instead participate in a kind of trial of strength with threats taking the place of physical contact and with an end in submission and flight.

Aggression, then, is not a common animal attribute. It is peculiarly human. Other animals do not make pyramids of the skulls of their enemies, nor do they erect coke ovens in order to exterminate those they consider inferior. They do no invent and manufacture instruments of torture. An anthropologist has remarked that "the extreme nature of human destructiveness and cruelty is one of the principal characteristics which marks off man, behaviorally, from other animals." William James had already pointed out that man is the most ruthlessly ferocious of beasts. Human aggression, then, can be distinguished from animal aggression by its violence and by its range and persistence. This fact is unfortunate for any moral prospects, and we shall have to look into it further. We shall want to ask first what human aggression is, next how it developed, and finally what it has led to.

II

If animals do not ordinarily exhibit aggression and humans do, what is peculiar about humans to make the difference? This is not at all clear, and, because it is not, I suggest a hypothesis of my own. When there are drives to reduce organ-specific needs — the needs, say, for water, food, a mate, information, activity, or security — the drives are not stopped when the needs are reduced. More water than necessary is stored, more food accumulated, more females collected, more activity undertaken, more information gained, more security sought — security which is ultimate rather than immediate. I call this phenomenon of leftover drives "excessive behavior." What does it suggest except one general implication: that the aim of every human male is to dominate permanently everything in his entire environment? The purpose of life is to stay alive, and, for man, this means that he seeks his security in terms of aggrandizement, through the incorporation within himself of as much of the external world as possible.

Excessive behavior is characteristically human behavior. It may be defined as the continuance of the drives beyond need reduction. And it serves to reduce a generic need for aggression rather than a specific need — the hunters who kill more animals than they can eat, the Don Juans who make love to more women than they can desire, the industrialists who accumulate more money than they can spend. But this kind of behavior has far more serious and extended import than we have seen thus far.

Let us expand the discussion by talking about a kind of generalized aggression which is unspecified with respect to alterable material objects; and let us assume that it is reducible in one of two ways: by destructive or by constructive acts. The drive to alter the environment accordingly may take the form of a short-range, an intermediate-range, or a long-range response. A word now about each.

Short-range response and the resultant action is violent, requiring a high state of arousal and ending in need reduction which is fast, effective, and complete. It is usually accompanied by a pleasurable sense of tension reduction which almost no other variety of response can provide. When a woman allows a man to make love to her, she effectively reduces his sexual needs; but he has others: the need for coercive aggression, for instance, which rape alone could satisfy. Easy access to the materials requisite for particular need reductions frustrates the generic need for aggression.

In rapid movement, the musculature dominates the organism and blankets all other needs. Life is action and living at its fullest may be, at least in one of its forms, furious and violent. Many of those who have been in battle often testify to the fact that there is no satisfaction to be compared with it. Certainly the popularity of war owes its existence to the need for short-range, destructive aggression. Cannibalism, which has had such a venerable history, is more complicated than rape or war and is even better for the purpose of reducing the need for violent action.

The point is that only in destructive behavior do we find a sufficient resistance from the environment to offer quick need reduction to aggression. But there are many more ordinary varieties to be seen at almost any time. Crimes and acts of violence, such as suicides, are common enough; but national hatreds, race hatreds, and prejudices are so prevalent that society may almost be said to be structured of them.

The destructive character of short-range actions has effects which are chiefly negative and antisocial. Destructive activity is often given a constructive interpretation by the man of action. He claims to be clearing the way for his own constructions when he destroys those of others, but hostility is certainly involved. The needs of the muscles, the drive to do, can be reduced more efficiently and more completely through violence. What it takes centuries to build can be destroyed in an instant, and destruction is more effective than construction as a need-reducing agent. The strongest evidence is contained in the fact that the heroes of history are the war lords, the Genghis Khans, the Alexanders, the Caesars, the Napoleons, the Lincolns. The men best remembered and celebrated are those who succeeded in getting the largest number of people killed. Wars occur with such frequency, and the reasons given for them are so various, that their causes must be traceable to a more fundamental physiological source. Men say they fight to win territory, to right a national wrong, to defend or spread a religion, to make the world safe for democracy; but there is the imminent possibility of conflict and often the recurrence.

Intermediate-range response is the most familiar variety, and its resultant actions are commonly regarded as the norm. In the main, it is constructive. It erects buildings, establishes institutions, accumulates cities, promulgates laws, and in general is the work of the peacetime leaders, the artists and scientists, the architects and politicians, through whose efforts men cooperate in construction of one sort or another. Intermediate-range actions are actions on a daily basis on which businesses are operated, medicine practiced, law cases tried, clothing worn, children conceived, and friendships conducted. Most human behavior is on this level.

It is not customary to consider intermediate-range response as a kind of aggression, but so it is. If, as we have said, aggression is the drive to dominate the environment, then altering the material environment in a constructive way, just as much as destroying it, is an attempt to dominate it. The intermediate-range response has an effect which is felt more slowly than the immediate results obtained by the short-range response, but it is genuine just the same.

Long-range response works even more slowly than intermediate-range, but it builds civilizations. Long-range actions, so pervasive and elusive, are difficult to detect and for practical purposes are usually not counted. But they have the most sustained continuity and, in the long run, involve the greatest effects, though such long-wave effects tend to go almost unnoticed. A man may design a new theory of social action while living and working in relative obscurity, but after his death his theory may be applied with all the violence of a revolution. Karl Marx read quietly in the British Museum Library, and there was no warning that his books would change the life of everyone in Russia and China. The movement from theory to practice may be likened to those "tidal waves" or *tsunami* which begin abruptly and travel enormous distances without attracting attention until they hurl themselves with tremendous force upon shore installations. Long-range action is constructive, but the accumulated events which over a protracted period amount to a construction are seldom recognized as such. Long-range action is that action which becomes an ingredient of all other action to the extent necessary to guide the sum total in a given direction.

Short-range muscular response represents the need to do in its purest form (although no such need is pure). Similarly, long-range muscular response involves being as well as knowing. The identification of the individual with a large or permanent object — such as a society — plays an important part. All moral behavior is long-range action, and it constitutes an effective need reduction, but not suddenly or all at once. The moral aim is nothing less than the construction of a good society, which is to say, a society in which all individual needs can be effectively reduced without mutual interference.

Long-range response involves a hierarchy of instructions according to which a sequence of operations is to be performed. Such a hierarchy may be called a plan.[6] A course of action so designed could be executed in a period lasting from, say, a day to an entire lifetime. Protracted intentions could require a very large number of long-delayed activities, so that short-range responses could be either indefinitely postponed or cancelled (but, in either case, frustrated). The plan is characteristic of the long-range response and may be either innate, as with the fixed-action patterns of the ethologists, or learned, as with the designs of the engineer or the budgets of the politicians.

The most important kind of plan for our purposes in this chapter is the established morality of a society as evinced by its customs, laws, and legal machinery: its law-makers, administrators, and courts. Here we have the definite and far-flung intention of the society to hold the behavior of its individual members within specific limits. Morality is not possible without immense social integration.

Many of the most magnificent of human achievements are the results of some degree of planning. To plan means for the individual to co-operate with other members of his society. The larger the unit — that is to say, the greater the amount of matter, the larger the volume of space, and the longer the extension of time — the more plans and long-range responses are required in order to participate, until finally we come to that socially cumulative and externally developed transmission apparatus, the epigenetic system of human culture.

III

Here, then, is the thesis toward which my argument has been tending. The paradox in man's development is the constancy of his opposite aims. He is at once a maker and a destroyer, and his behavior leads inevitably to both congruence and collision. Thus, despite the conflict involved, there must be some common mechanism. The alternation of war and peace, for example, would seem to point to important relations between them. Wars destroy so much of what was painfully constructed during periods of peace that the two seem at odds. Yet is this entirely the case? Intervals of peace usually last longer than periods of war, probably because men need time in which to rest and recuperate before engaging in more of such violent and costly actions. Yet there must be elements native to the time of peace which accumulate until war becomes inevitable and necessary. Let us see if it is possible to isolate these elements and determine their nature.

Social life always involves for the human individual a certain amount of both cooperation and competition. Cooperation means that competition must be restricted somewhat and conducted strictly in accordance with an established set of ground rules. But competition by the rules is limited and, therefore, the occasion for a whole host of frustrations. These can accumulate slowly until the total reaches unbearable levels. The sedentary life is also a source of frustration which in time must build up to the point where aggression becomes necessary. Thus there arises a need for violent action which the life of civilized man does not reduce except in war.

At the present stage of civilization, peace is a war that nobody wins. The opposing sides stand poised to do battle, but neither is strong enough to be sure of victory. Hence, it becomes safe (temporarily) for the individual to go routinely about his business, secure in the knowledge that a more open conflict has been postponed.

In this way, man finds himself with ambivalent drives and activities. His goals are to help and to hurt his fellows. He alternates these drives in such a way that competition becomes as common as cooperation, war as common as peace, hatred as common as love, egoism as common as altruism. Thus, for example, the individual carves out a fortune for himself — and then gives it away, as Carnegie in fact did. Or nations undertake to destroy each other, with the victor helping its former enemies to recover, even going so far as to make common cause with them against their former allies as, for instance, the United States did with Germany and Japan. I am reminded of the Nazi storm trooper who politely assisted the old lady into the van which was to take her to the gas chamber, and of those who resort to the use of force to convince others of the supremacy of brotherly love.

IV

How did man develop such an ambivalent pattern of behavior? To answer this question, we must look at his history and more especially at prehistory, taking as long a view of the past as possible.

The earliest hominids, the Australopithecines and the later Pithecan-thropines, living millions of years ago, were carnivores and cannibals. Hunting, especially the hunting of the large animals whch existed then, required some social cooperation and group activity; and, of course, cannibalism itself is seldom an individual enterprise. The later Neanderthalers, living between 200,000 and 40,000 years ago, were also cannibals and hunters.

In order to survive, early man had to raise families and kill large animals for food. Both of these enterprises involved social cooperation, and social cooperation had as its precondition the exercise of some control of aggression. Instead of fighting over game and mates, man learned how to divide all the food and the women. Thus, in order to prevent mutual extermination, morality came into existence.

Man, in his present constitution, is estimated to have been alive no more than 400,000 years. Of this 400,000, he hunted for more than the last 100,000. Agriculture was started only 10,000 years ago, a startling fact when you consider that civilization, literally the establishment of city life, was made possible only with agriculture and is, therefore, little older. Both agriculture and city life require a much larger degree of social cooperation than the activities of the lonely nomadic hunter. But you cannot reasonably expect all the effects to come from the bunched latter end in such a skewed distribution. Man came to his peaceful sedentary existence and submitted to the augmentation of modern metropolitan pressures, aggravated by a fabulous increase in population, when conditioned for it only by the hundreds of thousands of years of hunting and cannibalism which lay behind him. He seems to have been strongly shaped by his method of obtaining food before he was suddenly called upon to change.

One of the chief, recent consequences of living in large cities has been the development of more efficient methods for obtaining need reductions through complex social organizations and an increase in the knowledge of nature: the rise of industrialism and of scientific technologies. The beginnings of civilization were made when man had his own beginnings, and perhaps both in the same way. When the hominids came down from the trees onto the broad savannas, what had been chiefly a life based on brachiating arms and fructiferous diet was replaced by bipedal locomotion, upright posture, the use of hands, material tools, speech, and a carnivorous diet.

Once man learned how to use tools and languages (which are, after all, only a particular kind of tool, namely, that kind which is used for communication) his immediate destiny was fixed: he was compelled thenceforth to adapt himself to them. The humanization of the man-apes probably consisted in the process of externalization: learning how to do outside the body what had formerly been done only inside it. This constituted an immense advance in efficiency. The efficiency can be observed in two dimensions: intensive and extensive. The intensive dimension can be exemplified by cooking, which is a kind of external predigestion. The external dimension can be exemplified by writing, which is a kind of externalized speech. In these ways we can eat things, and we can say things over great distances in space and time, which would not otherwise have been possible.

Thus when man entered upon his civilized period, he brought with him an ambivalence of motivation. He worked with some of his fellows to obtain food, and some of the food he obtained were his fellows; not the same ones, it is true, but of the same species. He carried with him into civilization this ambivalence of motivation, and we can easily see it still at work today. Only he is expected to manage his need reductions under conditions quite different from those which existed when they were shaped. He loves — and hates — his fellowmen; and so he makes common cause with them — and also attacks them. He works with some and against others; and the picture is not made any clearer by the fact that the lines defining cooperation and competition keep shifting and reforming continually. This indicates an awkwardness and an unfamiliarity as well as an inheritance of ambivalence; but we are led toward a number of conclusions.

V

The first of these conclusions is that in all the years since man emerged from his prepongid and prehominid ancestors, there has been no progress in motivation, only in intensification. He has become much cleverer about getting what he wants, but he wants the many things he always wanted.

The second conclusion is that civilization is very recent — in anthropological terms it dates from only yesterday — and so its nature is highly experimental. We cannot be certain whether it will last. The development of nuclear weapons poses this last question in somewhat acute form, but the question itself had been posed already.

The third conclusion is that since civilization itself is not a very stable affair, neither man's artificially constructed material environment nor man himself exists in any promising state of equilibrium. And so the future of man is very much in doubt. Will his evolution continue at a very much accelerated rate or will he regress under the influence of nuclear-induced genetic damage?

Sir Julian Huxley[7] has argued that human evolution comes to a standstill because now man has made his own artificial environment. But the facts lead to precisely the opposite conclusion. For man has made his own environment, it is true, but he has not learned how to control that environment. He does not know what he wants to do with it, and he would be at a loss even to predict what its effect will be on him.

Furthermore, this artificial environment for which he is responsible is changing more rapidly than the natural environment ever did. Who can safely say what the industrial culture of megalopolitan man will look like in the next thousand years if the present tendencies are allowed to extrapolate unchecked? If man is adapted to his environment, and no less so when it is an artificial one, then if that environment is changing as rapidly as it seems to be doing, his adaptations will have to follow. For man is certainly conditioned by his own constructions: by his tools and by his languages. The violinist is a function of the violin, the pilot a function of the airplane, and not the reverse.

It is difficult to say at this point what the future holds, now that man has learned how to take still another hand in his own development. Recent discoveries in molecular biology point to the possibility that he will be able to plan his own genetic development. But what sort of human does he want to develop — perhaps I should ask, what sort of human should he want to develop?

Just now the answer to that all-important question is lacking. Certainly he is very far from achieving the kind of stability long possessed by the cockroach or the horseshoe crab, which are either so perfectly adapted to their environment or so internally strong as not to need such adaptation in order to survive (for the earth has changed materially in the millions of years during which these creatures have remained the same). But the importance of the question of genetic goals is with us still. If man could design his own progeny, what features would he want to build in them? Consider in this connection, for instance, the concept with which we started: the dual nature of aggression. Leave out the aggressiveness, then expect no achievement; leave in the aggressiveness, then count on more destruction.

If Julian Huxley is wrong, then human evolution has not come to an end. From ape to man is what we see looking back; and we tend to regard evolution only by looking back, for that is the flattering direction. But looking forward we see another prospect, that of the moralization of man. It could be achieved through the next stage in the process of evolution, which is to be from man to superman, not the superman of Nietzsche's *Zarathustra* nor yet that of our comic strips, but a moral superman who would exhibit virtues as much beyond our powers as ours are beyond those of the apes.

There are some hopeful signs that the moralization of man not only has begun but will continue and increase, and we may take a little courage from them.

One sign is the phenomenon of the social conscience developed in western European countries in the nineteenth century, according to which altruism is considered the only decent impulse, and the torture and killing of men wrong. Admittedly, tortures and killings still exist, but there is nothing new about that. What is new is the strong tone of disapproval which everyone has begun to share.

A second sign is the success of the democracies in reconciling opposite views. Rationalism and liberalism show themselves at their best in the degree to which the tolerance of differences is sustained. For where there is the tolerance of differences, there is apt to be that richness of values which promises progress in the kind of slow constructions of high culture which make civilized life desirable.

A third and last sign (though by no means as unmixed as the first two) is the recognition that the cost of wars conducted with nuclear weapons might be annihilation. Such a cost has been generally recognized and probably accounts for the fact that there has been no nuclear conflict to date. It may just be so expensive that it will have to be prevented, though for myself I think this is whistling in the dark past Cape Canaveral.

The chief human problem arising from the ambivalence of aggression is to learn how to build constructive substitutes for that kind of aggression which is reducible now only by means of destructive acts. William James understood this very well, but his solution was characteristic of his polite and genteel sheltered society. He wanted to send Harvard undergraduates to summer camps. Bertrand Russell in his Nobel Prize acceptance speech suggested providing rivers with rocky and dangerous rapids near all the large cities for those who feel the need for such a challenge. So you see that the solutions have not matched the difficulties. And that is why there are still wars. Wars are not only prevalent, they are, if anything, on the increase, and they are so mechanized and so dangerous that they threaten human survival.

Here, then, is the problem. We have developed the cooperative and constructive side of human nature to a point where it clashes severely with the competitive and destructive side. In other words, we have reached an impasse where we regard as morally wrong what can easily be accounted for biologically. What are we to do about this human species which is in some ways so admirable that its existence seems worth preserving? An answer will have to be found either by the psychologists through the control of motivation or by the practical moralists through the control of the epigenetic material culture. At the present reading, these approaches seem to be the most promising.

CHAPTER X

FROM HEGEL TO TERRORISM

Traditional logic as the criterion of truth has always found itself unable to cope with the brute facts of existence because conflicts present themselves as obstacles standing in the way of the logical requirements of consistency. Th evidence is strong enough: individuals, for instance, only too often behave in a contradictory fashion, societies are torn apart by oppositions of all sorts, while nature itself does not seem to be as moral as we might wish.

Plato tried to solve this problem by insisting that there is a domain of logic superior to the world of matter, but others preferred to pursue the possibility of unity. Aristotle, for instances urged that if the conflicts in the material could not be incorporated in logic, then perhaps logic could be incorporated in the material world. Both traditions have been continued intermittently ever since, and both have been considered unsatisfactory.

The most successful attempt to solve the problem was the realism which assumes that there are two separate but related domains, those of logic and matter, respectively, which are equal with regard to reality; but the issues have never seemed important to philosophers, not as important, say, as the theory of knowledge proposed by Kant or the theory of the dialectic argued by Hegel.

Not that the realistic tradition has been neglected in our own time; it was advocated by Peirce and Whitehead, among others. A high value should be placed on it beacause it is capable of containing not only the classical topics of metaphysics but also the important new findings of the physical sciences; yet a nagging question must inevitably arise. Why is this tradition now considered to lie so far outside the current fashions in philosophy as to seem nearly unrecognizable? One possible answer is that it makes too great a demand on philosophers whose interests do not normally include an understanding of the method or the discoveries in astronomy, physics, chemistry, and biology.

Into this predicament, which had been around since the Greeks, Hegel was able to move with his peculiar version of the dialectic, which gave a description of accidental alternation parading as a new kind of logic, but was in fact only a name for the wayward course of events as it zigzagged from one direction to another. In this way, he made what might otherwise have been considered disreputable actions seem called for by rationality. As a result, the heritage of Hegel was that anything can be justified as logical if its opposite can.

Consider some of the consequences of such a monstrous conception. If according to the dialectic the opposite of anything is necessary to it, then it follows that evil is necessary to good and error necessary to truth (as if there were only one evil corresponding to every good and one error to every truth!) This makes a hash of rationality, in the grand sense established for it by Plato and Aristotle, and a hopeless foolishness of any idealism; and, worst of all, justifies those who prefer the bad, the false, and the ugly to the good, the true, and the beautiful.

Thus it happens that ever since Hegel's philosophy was first published it has been a threat to mankind, for it makes destruction necessary. The dialectic is not logic, though it looks like logic, sounds like logic, and is in fact called logic. Marx saw in it the opportunity to defend any revolution he wished to mount by giving it a kind of rational justification.

There is little doubt that the success of Marxism in Asia has had its impact on philosophy in Europe and America. All of the conventional perspectives have had to be readjusted, all of the judgments revalued. At first sight it might appear that nothing has been changed, but actually there has been an unacknowledged shift of emphasis: narrow conceptions mistaken for wider ones, and small philosophies which were quite appropriate to special situations confused with those which are much larger. Some significant developments were even overlooked because they did not at first glance seem to bear on the main points. Clearly, there will have to be a reassessment in order to restore the balance.

The Marxists have been allowed to describe materialism in such a way that their alternative appears to be the only one. but materialism, when considered as part of metaphysical realism, can be neglected only by doing damage to the total picture. I hope, therefore, to show its current place in a comprehensive philosophy, for while it occupies a rightful position there, by itself it is not complete.

In a word, the greatest mistake made by western philosophy in recent decades was to allow the Marxists to preempt materialism so that rejecting Marxism has been allowed to mean rejecting materialism also. The official adoption of Marxism by the Soviet Union and by its satellites and China made some kind of dissociation from materialism necessary when it became so obvious that Marxism was a false philosophy. The error lay in supposing that because Marxism is materialistic, all materialism is necessarily Marxist.

Marxism hangs upon the theory that everything can be adequately explained by tracing the antagonism between social classes to its source in the ownership of the means of material production. The 'materialism' that Marx and Engels were talking about was the one advocated by Feuerbach in the nineteenth century, unchanged since it was first presented to the world by Leucippus and Democritus in the fifth century B.C. This is manifestly an absurd holdover, especially when one remembers that the physical sciences in the last century have provided a much richer and more complex knowledge of matter, so rich in fact that its components have not yet been exhaustively investigated. Putting together the constituents of the atom as disclosed by particle physics and the large-scale structure of the universe as disclosed by astronomy presents a different picture of matter, one hardly deducible from the factory system of production of Marx's day. There is no reason, therefore, to abandon materialism because of its outdated use by the Marxists.

If Hegel made the dialectic into a substitute for logic, and Marx saw the opportunity to combine it with materialism in order to defend the rightness of social revolution, then the French development in the early twentieth century was in some ways the most astounding of all: the moral justification of terrorism.

Remembering that both Marxist materialists and British idealists derived from Hegel, the French evidently thought the obvious choice for them was to develop another side of his philosophy. (No one seems to have considered the possibility of ignoring Hegel!) Alexandre Kojève (Kotjenikov), who taught in Paris from 1933 to 1939 at the *Ecole Pratique des Hautes Etudes*, and who was fortunate to have among his pupils the leading French intellectuals, men like Raymond Aron, Jacques Lacan, and Maurice Merleau-Ponty, advanced a "terrorist conception of history." Kojève's "political cynicism" enabled him to "compromise philosophy" by "advocating the virtues [sic] of massacre and violence" through the pursuit of "the unreasonable origins of reason."[1]

Kojève was responsible for much in the writing of his French contemporaries, and certainly for the element of radicalism that most of them displayed. He brought out more clearly than anyone the inherent destructiveness that Marx found in Hegel, and in his lengthy treatise interpreting Hegel, he may have been softening up the French for a takeover by the Marxists. All of the elements were present to support such a suspicion. It certainly did have that effect on Sartre, who associated fraternity with terror, proposed nausea as an acceptable basis for the philosophy of life, and flirted with communism. And it must have had the same effect on Merleau-Ponty, who in his *Humanism and Terror* (1947) defended the Moscow Trials against the criticism of them by Arthur Koestler in his *Darkness at Noon,* arguing that state terror could be justified in the interests of the revolutionary future.

Marx himself had shown the way, of course. The corrupting influence of Hegel's *Logic* had not been noticed until Marx chose to rely upon it. The primary importance of the concept of opposition came to Kojève from Hegel, and violence is always involved in extreme versions of opposition. As late as 1968, Kojève was still "reported to have said that, since there had been no bloodshed, nothing had happened," and he claimed that "bloody strife and not 'reason' is responsible for the progress of events toward the happy conclusion."[2]

Evidently, philosophy can be the name for any point of view whatsoever provided only that it is stated and defended abstractly, and the French, who are an intellectual people, are always at home among abstractions. They were quick to grasp and solve the difficulties presented by organizing such a conception as a program. More recently, the French have seen how they could use it to justify their defection from the traditional values. It is a peculiarity of the French that their devotion to reason always exceeds any question of what they are defending by reason. This narrow conception of rationality has led them into some strange avenues of thought. Defeated in two world wars which were yet won by their allies, the French decided that if they could no longer lead western civilization, then at the very least they could bring it down, and in Hegel they found the proper intellectual base to justify their destructive actions.

The example of Kojève is capable of teaching a curious moral. To make the point, I will have to be permitted an aside to examine one serious flaw in the history of logic, a flaw which went unnoticed though it had deep roots in Aristotle's version. Systems of logic have been judged entirely in terms of the criterion of consistency. If conclusions follow from premises, logic, it has been believed, can call for nothing more, and therefore validity is all that has been required of logical systems. The difficulty arises only when it is asked what a logical system is expected to include. Is there any demand for comprehensiveness? Is there, in other words, any requirement that everything relevant to a system be included in it?

Hegel correctly perceived the weakness of logic so far as its applications were concerned: that it did not add the criterion of completeness to that of consistency. Applied logic, which could call only on consistency, could not account for the movements of matter that are required by energy. A second criterion was needed and completeness could supply it.

What is named completeness here must be distinguished from the contemporary use of the term in mathematical logic. In logic, "a deductive system is complete if all the desired formulas can be proved within it,"[3] and "anything true is provable."[4] These are admittedly logical criteria, but for a philosophical system the meaning is quite different, so different that the use of the same term can only be a source of confusion. Completeness for a philosophical system (as contrasted with a logical system) means simply that *anything which belongs in the system must be included in the system*, a much broader criterion, but one intended for a much broader system. Logic specifically excludes anything which is non-logical, whereas in philosophy nothing that *is* can be excluded.

There was, in short, a difference here which Hegel was quick to exploit. Opposites do not have the logical limitations that contradictories have, and so he replaced the latter with the former. This made it possible for him to describe, in his "logic" of the dialectic, what happens in the material world of conflict, certainly a valuable addition to philosophical explanation even though one that made difficulties for the logician.

Armed with this distinction, let us return to Kojève. What he did — and by extension, his French followers — was to try to construct a philosophy within the limits of a *logical* system but having the inclusiveness of a *philosophical* system. If they had succeeded, they might have seen that their result was absurd, and they would in that case not have made the mistake of supposing that a viable society could be based on the endorsement of terrorist tactics.

If they had pursued the logical analogy, they might also have made the discovery that for the mathematical logician, "anything provable is true,"[5] whereas for the philosopher with his comprehensive system this is not the case. The error lay in the ambiguous use of the term 'truth': what is provable in a system is true *in that system* but not necessarily true to fact, since logical truth and factual truth are by no means one and the same. Philosophy has the task of embracing both, even though logic, like all pure mathematics, belongs to the domain of abstractions, while fact belongs to the world of material existence.

There has been considerable progress in realistic philosophy, but chiefly as the result of work by the physical scientists. They understand the need to do empirical research when it is suggested by provocative fact, and to put the findings together by recourse to pure mathematics. Thus the two domains are not only preserved separately but also properly related.

The situation did not go unnoticed by all philosophers, even though when the revolution in physics occurred at the turn of the twentieth century, their first reaction was to explain to the physicists the meaning of the new discoveries. It never occurred to the philosophers to consider what effect on philosophy those discoveries might have. Their attitudes were dictated by a deepseated belief in the superiority of philosophy. The first result of the encounter of philosophy with modern science was to lay claim to superiority in matters of fact: philosophy was not prepared to surrender any corner of its turf. Yet when philosophers ventured to speculate on the facts, they were often wrong; it was not their province.

If the history of philosophy's encounter with science makes interesting reading, remember that the two disciplines have been engaged in the same enterprise: endeavoring to discover the nature of reality. No wonder that Descartes resorted to physiology when he declared that the place where the mental and the physical meet is the pineal gland, one which has only this year (1981) been more correctly described by the physiologists as the source of the hormone, melatonin. And no wonder either that Hegel declared the number of the planets to be seven, with the additional declaration that no more would be discovered, when the discovery of Ceres was announced. That is why the philosophers were prepared to take the time off from tending their own gardens to cultivate the gardens of others. That the situation could be reversed — that the philosophers could learn from the physicists a new way of looking at philosophy — never occurred to them.

Peirce and Whitehead were the principal exceptions. At the end of the nineteenth century and just before the revolution in physics effected by Planck, Einstein, and others, Peirce was perhaps the first philosopher to note the metaphysically realistic nature of the scientific method, with the equal reality of the two domains represented by experiment and mathematics. Whitehead in two books, *Science and The Modern World* and its systematic sequel, *Process and Reality,* tried to show what the new physics had to say that was fresh about the old categories of philosophy; but that feature of his work was not followed.

Whitehead's undertaking was a valiant effort, yet it has not been as influential as it might have been had his kind of knowledge of the sciences been the common experience of philosophers. Also, there have been great scientific advances since his day which require interpretation in a comprehensive philosophy if the whole relationship is to be brought up to date. In recent decades, the data from the physical sciences have been flowing in at such an amazing rate that only a bold investigator would dare to try putting it all together; yet that remains the obligation of the philosopher, who cannot afford to ignore any authentic and reliable knowledge from whatever quarter.

What emerges from this brief survey is the conclusion that a return to the realistic philosophy is necessary because it is the only one capable of reconciling the two domains. All that is needed is to bring both of them up to date, though admittedly this will require a considerable effort. Also, the theory of Hegel and his followers, the Marxists, must not be allowed to dominate the domain of matter by claiming its preeminence in the domain of logic. The proper balance must be restored, and logic, not the dialectic, returned to its rightful place as the arbiter of truth. Otherwise we shall all be destroyed, and the kind of civilization in which we were beginning to determine its direction by recourse to ideals will be lost to mankind for the foreseeable future.

CHAPTER XI

A RELIGION FOR
A NEW AND NON-MARXIST
MATERIALISM

There is more than a hint in the new knowledge of matter that the spiritual life of man need not be denied by empiricism, but instead can be expected, acknowledged, recognized, and understood. It ought to be possible to have a religious enterprise consisting of the effort of man to get in touch with the dominant inner quality of the universe. Since man himself derived from the objective world and continues to reflect it, a richness of diversity of values exists on both sides of the curtain of consciousness. Those values on the subjective side are a cultural selection made by society from the larger supply which belongs to the environment. The urge to identify the long-range self with an object sufficiently permanent to be worthy of such identification is a religious urge. And the size of the object is an index to the intensity of that urge. The larger the universe, the greater the longing for identification with it or its cause. The desire for the good of all the parts or for the beauty of the whole world is spiritual.

Everyone carries approximately the same weight of beliefs. The emotional charge is roughly equal, whether distributed among a few propositions or many. If faith is belief without reason, then everyone has access to that minimal faith which is faith in reason itself. But by and large, people find more satisfaction in spreading their beliefs thin and in holding to them absolutely: the less one believes in, the more one needs to believe in it. Great tensile strength is required to find sufficient support in the delicate, yet firm subscription to proximate guesses. Witness the "passionate sceptics" of the seventeenth century, witness Hume.

Any new religion which does not contradict the findings of science must recognize the paradox that ultimate knowledge seems to be reserved from us, but that nevertheless we seem committed to seek it. We can no more give up our efforts to discover the nature of the cosmos and its causes than we can discover them. The compromise seems to lie in a willingness to settle for the time being for conditioned and limited knowledge. We do know that we know; but our knowledge is not final. Thus the true religious enterprise is inquiry into the nature of reality, an inquiry in which the physical scientists for the moment lead, though they make no presumption to exclusivity.

Such an approach would definitely place the locus of religious interest in the future instead of in the past. All organized religions to date look backward to a founder, but there is no warrant that this is the only course, for it means that the source of our inspiration becomes daily more remote. It contradicts the direction of time's arrow; if there is to be a better life, it must lie ahead, for otherwise we become less and less holy as the recession of the year proceeds apace. Hope as well as piety lie in the future, when light might become better and more meaningful than it has ever been. A religion of materialism must learn to face forward.

The chief instrument with which to begin the inquiry is hypothetical reasoning. Tentative knowledge has its own form of expression: the language of probability. Statistical arguments do presuppose a background of hypothetical truths, yet these need not be asserted. The penumbra of assumptions is easier to change than the dogma contained in a creed. In religious inquiry, we should recognize that we are dealing with considerations involving possibilities and that the results of the inquiry can be treated in terms of the modal categories. As Rescher has it, the "function of the modal categories is to provide the machinery for an exact logical articulation of the informal idea of the 'relative degree of potential commitment' to the endorsement of statements, reflecting their priority-rating with respect to 'fundamentality' or 'importance'."[1]

The empirical criterion in terms of which the prospect of establishing a new religion for materialism might be explored is one which can be used to measure the older religions in an attempt to evaluate their accomplishments.

When we look to see what has happened, the first thing that strikes us is that the members of one religion have not fared any better than those of any other. They do not contract fewer diseases, they do not have less poverty, they are not less ignorant. If God has a favorite religion, we have been given no sign which one it is. We are justified in concluding, then, that so far as religion is concerned, God is unaffiliated. Men find religion comforting because faith is comforting and doubt a source of discomfort. But on this ground (even if on this ground alone), any religion will serve as well as any other, for all faiths are *equally* comforting. Thus no established religion seems to have any right to speak for religion as such in any exclusive sense.

When we ask which people are best off and why, we are struck by the fact that the determinant is not religion, but science. Technology, science, and its offspring, applied science, and the industrialism which results from these, seem capable of providing a better life in this world than any religion left on its own. Prosperity, longevity, health, and education, replace poverty, disease, and ignorance, in countries which have fostered science. Judged by these conditions, if the world is the result of the will of God, then it would seem that He prefers His people to pursue science rather than religion.

The one blot on this picture is the continuance of the phenomenon of war. Science has developed the instruments of war to a dangerous point, but religions were responsible for as many wars as any other institution, wars as widespread, as ferocious, and as indiscriminate. On this score, then, there is nothing to choose between religion and science; so far as peace is concerned, there is. The by-products of science, through applied science and technology, could make for a better world, certainly one with more food and better living conditions generally. And if religion claims that it provides immortality, the empirically oriented could reply that the case is yet to be demonstrated. We know no more of what, if anything, happens after death than we did at the outset of such speculations many hundreds of thousands of years ago.

Religion and science share equally in leading to the best and the worst in human affairs: the best, in providing solace and material welfare respectively; the worst, in providing holy wars and the atom bomb. For the truth is that regardless of the type of institution which is dominant, a church or a scientific establishment, there has been no progress in motivation. Ambivalence is the name of the human game, which is both to help some and to hurt others.

Materialism is not inconsistent with the belief that some material events, such as the shaping of symbols which point toward the limits of matter and the craving of human organisms for identification with large, faraway, and enduring objects, to say nothing of the feelings of exaltation which accompnay such cravings, indicate the existence of a passionate curiosity about the whole material universe and its possible cause. All that materialism should do (as contrasted with what it does) is oppose the claim of some men to extra-material authority for the exercise of the control over other men. If reality be defined as equality of being, then no material part of the whole universe is any more authentic or closer to the whole than any other part. But also, every part is an authentic part. Everything and everyone is saved or damned together, in the intimate and unlimited community of formed material.

What is religious feeling? It can be described as exalted emotions implicit in the craving for long-range persistence, arising from identification with faraway objects representing the size and permanence of the universe, and seeming to bring us in this way closer to its cause. Such a craving is disclosed by the inclination toward a belief in immortality despite the absence of any evidence derived from experience.

It is worthy of note that great art can do as much as can be done to transport the individual beyond his petty concerns into a glimpse of those values which may exist at the level of the whole universe; and worthy of note, also, is that many of the more successful of the older religions have always taken advantage of this fact, though the implications of such support have never been noticed. Thus a material version of mysticism is possible on the basis of what we know about matter and have learned to do with it, a mystical materialism which is able to justify religious feelings.

We should not have to go beyond the material universe, then, in order to account for religious responses. As with Spinoza, the spiritual can be provided for without designating a special category. It can be accomodated by attention to the activities of materials which in some contexts are directed toward the limits of matter. Some recognition of the immense extent of the universe is all that is needed to make us feel its essentially religious nature.

What lies between the cause of the universe and the universe itself are its limits: what are these, where do they stand, and what do they mean? The most religious undertakings currently being pursued are those in the physical sciences, the exploration of the components of the universe and their dimensions and constructions. Here is no idle mysticism invoked by means of the deliberate cultivation of abnormal subjective states, through fasting, prolonged prayer, or some other mechanism for promoting feelings of ecstasy. Here, instead, is a mystical materialism, produced by facts and elaborated by reasons, on the basis of the objective world as observed by the scientists.

Modern astronomy has made the individual increasingly aware of the immensity of the cosmos. The millions of planets orbiting the suns in our Galaxy, and the vast system of millions of galaxies, dwarf human petty existence and threaten to rob it of meaning. How puny seems man and all his efforts, how feeble, how very unimportant.

And yet, need that be the correct reading? The evaluation of a given body of evidence and the determination of just what hypothesis that evidence supports is the most delicate and easily distorted of all empirical undertakings. Could one not, for example, come logically to the opposite view? Civilization itself, we learn from archeological and geological studies, is hardly more than 10,000 years old; how very short a time that is compared even to life on earth! We and all our works will, in all likelihood, be swept away into the debris of the next interglacial loess. Yet does the very fact that the emergence of man coincides with the end of the last ice age not mean that we are looking at an event horizon beyond which we cannot see, but which might be concealing a wealth of previous civilizations? Has it not all been done before, and the traces obliterated?

The record is far from clear. From the profusion of nature, for instance, millions of sperm cells produced for every one that fertilizes an egg, we should be able to conclude that no individuals count for more than any others. But if there is not a special destiny in the split-second life of the merest meson, then all was lost from the beginning and there is no sense to anything. The significance of human destiny rides on every infinitesimal shred of being as much as it does on sharing in the fate of the infinitely large meta-galaxy.

There is nothing in the human individual that need perish forever. His cells, his organs, even the peculiar arrangement of the organism which gives him his uniqueness, exist as potential when they are not actual. And so its not inconceivable from biological knowledge that he could occur again.

It is not through participating in the longest survival, but having had a place in history at all that holds the greatest hope. For the shortest existence is as much authentic existence as is the longest. We compete not through activity so much as through understanding, and our brief visit here on earth has the import of intensity, if not the grandeur of extensity. We cannot ever achieve an effect comparable to a colliding galaxy, but we can know about it, and that is perhaps second only to the event itself.

It would not be inconsistent with materialism to suppose that there is no reason at all why there is matter. For it is entirely possible that being is an effect without a cause. Failing that, where we know the effect and not the cause, we can reason from effect to cause and assert that the effect must have been the effect of a cause, and therefore, that there must have been a cause; but this gives use no license to assert dogmatically whether there was a cause or what that cause was, if it was. There can be no conclusion to the whole from the behavior of the parts.

It does seem as though the more important a topic is, the less we know about it. Science has nothing to say for or against the idea of a creator. It studies the created world and leaves open the question of whether the world was created, and if so, how; there is no evidence. Any evidence for the creation of the world would have to lie outside that world in an area where science never ventures.

An explanation of the universe may exist, and the human mind may, at the same time, be incapable of comprehending it. Kant was right in his claim that we only can experience what our limited powers allow, and these powers confine us to the world disclosed by the senses and confirmed by reason. All transcendental knowledge, that is to say in Kant's terms knowledge beyond experience, is acquired by means of analogy, and all analogy is limited where applicable at all.

The best we can do, then, is to argue from the world of God, and if need be, also from God to the world. If God *is* the cause of the world, what is that world like? We can study the effects in order to learn something about the cause, if indeed it took that sequence. If the world is the will of God and whatever happens does so in accordance with His intentions, then the most religious interest we could have is in the world. We can learn nothing about God through mere speculation on the concept, but we could learn about the world, for, as Galileo pointed out long ago, nature is the book of God.

We are justified in asserting, then, on the basis of our powers, that we mean no more by religious undertakings than the exploration of the limits of the world. God stands at the limits, or, if not, then is represented in our inquiries by those limits. We can say no more, though it is much that we have said when we have said this. Peirce was convinced that a passive and indiscriminate attitude of sensible receptivity would result in "The perception of...manifold diversity of specificalness in general" and that this would amount to "a direct, though darkling, perception of God." His name for it was "musement."[2]

The intricacy, the complexity, the unity and diversity of the visible world certainly do point to a completeness and a harmony. What is usually meant by a belief in a god or gods is faith in the essential rightness of things, a rightness upon which man feels he can afford to rely when his efforts to probe into the meaning of his brief and painful existence fail.

Supernaturalism is not truly essential to the conception of God. There is a God of naturalism, too. Activity does not disclose His presence; we are left with sense experience and reason. But God is neither a sense object nor an abstract idea. Since there is insufficient evidence either way, the whole topic must remain in the form of a question.

Those who speculate concerning nature do not give up their activity when their observations and thoughts approach the limits of nature. And the limits of nature may be as close as it is possible to approach to the reason of nature. There is no necessity to consider that the only way to see nature as a whole is to look down upon it from above; there is also an inclusive system to be observed by looking out as far as possible along the surface.

If we know anything about the universe, it is that all things in it are connected. The limits of nature are to be found in two directions: toward the largest whole, which is the meta-galactic system of cosmology; and toward the smallest parts, which are those studied in particle physics. Is this not, after all, what we mean by the holy: that there is a unity to the universe, that all material objects consist of the same set of entities, and that all obey the same laws? Yet implicit here also is the idea that there must be a diversity to unify, that without differences there could be no movement toward unity. And so the unity is not primal unity with unreal Parmenidean or Hegelian parts, but a unity of a real whole composed of real parts whose differences are as real as their similarities. But if all things in the universe are *equally* parts of the universe whatever other unequal properties they may or may not possess, then this equal participation is what is meant by the holy, and that person is most responsive to the holy who is most sensitive to this fact.

The greater part of the time an individual spends on human affairs is occupied with earning a living, raising a family, relaxing with friends. Religion does not need to be maintained as a special enterprise, but can be the determining factor in how he conducts the ordinary business of life. A religious attitude rightly understood (which is to say, accurately comprehended intellectually and accepted by feeling) is not a question of how clearly one sees his religion, but rather of how clearly by means of it one sees everything else.

It is possible to specify something of the proper approach. The flexibility of belief called for by the new conception of the natural world requires balancing attachment with non-attachment, seeking an unaffiliated truth, practising active non-interference, maintaining half-belief, having reverence for everything, exercising standpointlessness, and reasoning from the Unknown God. It calls for staying on the positive side, making a dogma of fallibilism, preferring safeguards to rules, and holding no beliefs beyond inquiry.

CHAPTER XII

ON HATRED

No one ever achieved fame and fortune by offering an unflattering portrait of the human species, an activity which evidently must serve as its own reward; and indeed will have to function in that capacity for the philosopher, who ought to be, even if he is not always, devoted to the discovery of the truth, wherever it is found. All facts are by nature true, and whatever theories are not in accord with them will have to go. This still leaves standing a considerable residue of rival theories differing in perspective only to the degree to which they are inclusive.

The fact is that man is the wolf of man: that quite apart from the harsh natural conditions of existence, to say nothing of its brevity and often painful end, the blazing hatred of some individuals and social groups for others is responsible for much of the damage done to them and the agony suffered by them. This has often been mentioned in passing, but because it is a disagreeable set of facts always has been quickly forgotten, so that none of its consequences were ever as thoroughly examined as its critical nature warrants. The American thinker, Charles S. Peirce, once observed that he who wishes to affect the future cannot paint the ground in front of him. It is in this spirit, perhaps, that the topic of hatred has been avoided, even though its vivid presence and drastic consequences were never far afield.

If events as reported in the daily newspapers are at all representative, hatred is all around us, making a sharp contrast with the love with which it is invariably associated as a pair of opposites. Love and hate are often mentioned together at the outset of discussions about the nature of love, but we prefer to devote our thoughts to ideals in the very midst of activities which contravene them; chiefly, I suppose, because our images of ourselves cannot bear comparison with our actions. We are not engaged in carrying out our ideals, only in espousing them abstractly.

Many volumes and thousands of journal articles have been devoted to the explanation of love in all of its various forms, but far less energy has been spent on hate. This is a curious fact, especially when it is remembered that hate accounts for human behavior as much as love does.

Hatred is common enough, yet it is not always so clear or obvious why someone or something is hated, often not even to the hater. Most hatreds are caused by rivalries and by competition and the like; but there are also those which cannot be traced to any occasion or cause: they just *are*. When William Blake wrote

> I do not like thee, Dr Fell,
> The reason why, I cannot tell,
> I do not like thee, Dr Fell

he was expressing just such an emotion. Although it must be true that we always think we can justify our behavior, it does not follow that its cause is always known. Nietzsche wrote in *Zarathustra*, "I have long ago forgotten the reasons for my opinions," "and," he might have added, "for my emotions."

In a book on esthetics, I argued some time ago that beauty could not be understood without a prior understanding of the ugly.[1] Now, by analogy, I would like to show that love cannot be understood without a prior understanding of hate, which is its positive opposite. Hate is positive because it calls for action: the destruction of the hated object. (The contradictory of hate is not love, but non-hate.) Hate is a more common motive for action than love because it is more intense, immediate, and final.

Ethologists have pointed out that all species live by killing, and that such aggressiveness is not confined to predators, but exists even among herbivores. "Bulls attack other bulls. Cocks have even become symbols of aggressiveness"[2] Elsewhere I have joined the group of thinkers who hold that man inherited his aggressiveness, and I have tried to show its positive side by defining aggression as the desire to alter something in the environment by force, thus making construction as much a form of aggression as destruction.[3]

Hatred is, after all, only aggression seen subjectively. Thanks to the physiological needs, it is an expression of appetitive behavior before the fact, and aggression is sure to follow it. Hate, which can occur as the conscious recognition that a need has been frustrated, is not an end but an emotion on the way to an end: a negative element which must be surmounted before the need can be reduced.

Hatred, then, is the result of frustrated aggression, and this holds true of all the forms it takes: anger, rage, wrath. The act of aggression is usually need-reducing; the destruction of the object removes the motive for hate, and thus also eliminates the hate itself. Now since aggression in one form or another is built into the human organism, which must alter material objects in its immediate environment either through construction or destruction if it is to survive, and since aggression cannot always accomplish its aims, hate must continue to be an essential ingredient of human life.

However, much of aggression does not involve hate. The individual who kills to eat does not hate the animal he kills, does not hate the trees he cuts down to build a house, does not hate the mate he impregnates in order to satisfy his sexual need. Hate can arise from all three of these occasions, but only when there is competition for them with other individuals. Other forms of frustration do not lead to hate; a man does not hate his prey because it escapes his weapon or the drouth which may destroy his trees, but he may hate the woman who goes off with another man. As a result, he may engage in actions which have nothing to do with need-reduction, but only with frustration. Hate is human, a response made by humans and prompted on some occasions by the existence or actions of other humans.

Despite the obvious analogy of humans to other animals, animals do not hate. The emotional life of an animal probably does not extend beyond the reduction of its immediate needs. A lion 'needs' the death of the wildebeest it kills in order to satisfy its hunger, and most likely no such emotion as hatred is ever involved, any more than the human individual hates the cow which is to provide his steaks. There is no carry over of the motive of aggression in animals. It has been noted many times that a lion after killing a wildebeest will eat it within range of the foraging animals who show no fear of the sated predator.

We are always confronted in the world with what William James called a busy, buzzing confusion and so have the task of sorting things out for ourselves. I suppose the implicit criterion for such a selection is what is good for us and what is bad, though the bald expression of such moral considerations is seldom recognized. Every individual has to make a different selection, and part of the equipment to help him to do so are his feelings. These are graded, from indifference to liking to loving, on the one side, and from mild distaste to dislike and hatred on the other.

To some extent, the emotions are independent and lead lives of their own. The more rational an individual, the more he knows what he is doing and why, but in most people the feelings prevail over the reasons: they live in such a superficial manner that their actions are prompted only by their feelings, and so most of the time they are in a state where on the slightest pretext, feelings rise to the degree of intensity called emotions. Everyone acts on impulse: in a certain sense, it is the only way to act; but the impulses of a rational individual are more defensible than the impulses of an irrational one.

Perhaps it would be better if all were left to reason to make the decisions, but that seldom happens, and the feelings are, for the most part, less gentle than reason might have been. With any sort of extended concentration, the feelings tend to go to extremes: love, or else hate. These are, of course, opposites and so lie close together: one can so easily turn into the other. A wife who loved her husband inordinately will hate him with equal intensity when he divorces her. If often seems as though such intensity of feeling is indifferent to the signs; a plus can become a minus so easily, though it does seem that it never happens the other way round: hate seldom, if ever, turns into love. That the degradation of the feelings seems a one-way process is significant in some way not yet properly analyzed.

It has as often been noted that there is in man an innate aggressive drive, without ever adding a comment on the biological function it represents. The basic human needs which serve survival are involved: the needs for water, food, a mate, and living space, to say nothing of ideas and exercise, all of which are dictated by specific organs. To reduce these needs, material objects in the environment must be altered in suitable ways. The aggressive drive is there to serve the others; without it, man would be so passive he would perish in a short time.

It is not my purpose here to expatiate on the human needs and drives, which I have endeavored to deal with in another place,[4] but rather to examine one of the emotions which accompany them. In the course of pursuing the objects which must be acquired to reduce the needs, obstacles are encountered. Very often these obstacles consist in other individuals on their way to the same goals. Such individuals must, if possible, be eliminated; but first they are hated, and if they prove stubborn, they are hated even more. Thus hatred has a more or less permanent, if undesirable, place in the human catalogue of activity and its consequent emotions.

Emotions in general, then, are the result of frustrated needs, the effects of drives which fail somehow to reach their goal-objects. They are the responses made by the whole organism to the blocking of intentional behavior, the effects of unsuccessful episodes of directed aggression. I am not suggesting what emotions are, only how they come about; what they are, of course, are felt needs. The emotion of hate is the repression of the impulse to eliminate the hated objects, and perhaps, to destroy it altogether.

Hate may be defined as the emotion which is characterized by anger. It is usually accompanied by the desire to inflict injury or accomplish destruction. It does not persist but instead recurs until its object is attained, and then it ceases abruptly. As an emotion, it may be short-lived — no one can sustain such an intensity of feeling for very long — but that does not mean it cannot be revived; indeed, the likelihood is that it will be, for it has laid down pathways which will be easier to traverse on each successive occasion. Attention, however, tends to lag when there is action, and so what is hated is hated in short bursts, prompted by reminders of the object.

The English language is rich in synonyms which express differences of meaning under cover of a general definition. When hate cannot be reduced by the destruction of its object, the emotion turns to the longer-range version. Albert Camus wrote to a German friend in 1943:

> The French are difficult on the subject of
> virtues. And they don't assume them unless they
> have to. This gives their wrath the silence and
> strength you are just beginning to feel.[5]

Camus made the educated assumption that what he felt about the Nazis was shared by his countrymen individually and collectively, and he was correct. Given sufficient social reinforcement, hate turns to wrath, an intense resentment capable of becoming rage when its expression by action against a hated object is not possible.

One reason for hate is rivalry, another and perhaps more common is the fact of difference. Racial, religious, and national differences seem quite enough to provide the kind of hatred which leads to wars. What we don't understand, we fear, and prolonged fear leads easily enough to hate. For a single interbreeding species like mankind, the differences in culture can be quite marked. We resent anyone who does ordinary things in what looks to us like extraordinary ways: using chopsticks instead of forks, sitting on the floor cross-legged instead of on chairs, speaking in a strange language — these are quite sufficient provocation to invoke hatred.

We forget, of course, how rapidly our own customs and institutions undergo radical revisions. It ought to be sufficient to consider only the change in sexual customs and overt morality from the middle of the nineteenth century to our own a hundred and forty years later. If we hate those who behave differently from us, just think how we would regard our immediate ancestors and — worse still — what they would have thought of us.

The ambivalence of motivation, the twin urges to help one's neighbors and to hurt them, means that every population contains disparate elements: those in whom self-sacrifice rises to the surface, and those who enjoy torturing others, and many circumstances contribute to the decision concerning which group shall gain control. No doubt, there are men of good will in Moscow, but I do not believe they can be found among the members of the secret police.

The two opposed motives are not always quite so separate. The love-hate relationship as a phenomenon is well known, and in the emotional life these two are often close together, with individuals oscillating between them. Hatred, in a word, is almost always somewhere in the picture in any complete description of the emotional life.

The drives to reduce basic needs exist among all animals, otherwise they could not survive; but in man there is one peculiarity: very often the drives persist when the needs have been reduced and may indeed continue long after. An animal stops hunting when it is no longer hungry but a man does not; he has learned to store supplies in excess of his need and to kill for the sheer pleasure of killing; and so *pari passu* with all of his other needs. Oriental potentates have collected women in harems far in excess of any possible sexual need. The rich strive to become richer, the powerful reach out for more power. An individual who succeeds in accumulating a fortune which is large enough to buy anything will continue, in most cases, to add to it. This tendency increases the hatred, for it brings individuals more into conflict with each other than they otherwise might have been.

In this way, the emotion of hate can exceed what is called out by a hated object. If animals modify their environment before submitting to its influence, which has the result that they are partly formed by it and exert limited control over their exchanges with it, then hatred has some effect upon the hater, an undesirable but necessary result of the initial act of hate. The leftover drive of hate can have an adverse effect upon the hater, up to the point of negating any effect he may exercise upon the hated object.

The analogy therefore has its well-defined limits. In human hate, there can be a huge carry over. A man will "harbor a grudge" for his entire lifetime if he has no opportunity to exercise it on the destruction of a hated object. Hence the feud.

Hatred can, of course, have positive as well as negative results when looked at in the round. Many constructive social effects can be the result of national fears and rivalries. It is doubtful whether the American space program would have been developed as quickly and as successfully if there had not been a race with the Soviets to the moon. Competition, which is responsible for so many positive achievements, often carries animosity with it. The leftover drives aggravate the rivalries, but there is some reason to suppose that civilization itself may be the result of leftover drives.

The enmity of individuals is a native product, but life is not entirely individual. It is social; institutions are necessary for common undertakings. Men and women are accordingly organized into institutions for various reasons; most have to do with the gaining of a livelihood; but there are a few which extend beyond that and which hold in view the prospect of the understanding of the nature of things and the possibility of continuance. The larger institutions, and often even the smaller ones, have to justify themselves with fundamental beliefs about reality if they are to receive mass support.

Let us use the cover term 'creed' to describe institutional philosophies, regardless of whether they are ambitious or modest. In this sense of the term, we may say that states and religions have creeds, but so also do fraternal associations and professional societies. In the larger organizations, such as governments and churches, the aim is to bring individuals together in a common enterprise. To some extent and for awhile this does happen; but then institutions of this nature tend to fall apart, and the creeds with which they started become the causes of violent opposition. I have only to cite the subdivisions of Hinduism, Christianity, and Islam to make my point; in at least the latter two cases, frequent wars have resulted.

Thus creeds have served to intensify hatreds rather than to eradicate them. Resting on absolute truths, or so their adherents suppose, each holds that his particular truth is the only one in existence, when the fact is that absolute truth is the cheapest and most prevalent commodity in the world: everybody has one. There might be less hatred in the world if the circumstances could be arranged so there were less claims for them. Creeds only serve to reinforce hatreds by giving them a justification which appears often erroneously to rest on reason.

In our own day, those who were witnesses to the Nazi holocaust even at a distance and who have been informed of the horrors of the Gulag Archipelago in the Soviet Union — which still go on today — are condemned to live in a world where such things can occur. All over the globe since the beginning of the present century, this has been the prevalent practice. No special region has a monopoly: in Africa, the Nigerians against the Ibos; in southeast Asia, the Cambodians against their own people; in the Middle East, the Arabs and Jews against each other; and above all, perhaps, in the preparation of world war III by the Soviets and the Americans.

If hatred was not strong in many people, these events could never have taken place. Even organized religions, with their responsive creeds which were supposed to promote the brotherhood of man, do very little in this direction, as the history of any 'world' religion amply demonstrates and is demonstrating still today in Ireland between Christians, and in Iran and Iraq between Moslems.

Ethologists often have overlooked the fact that prey and predators are not confined to the non-human animal world; they exist also and equally among humans who often flourish at the expense of other humans. This is as true of individuals as it is of social groups and nation-states. Among people, there are no sated predators. The heroes men admire are those who have conquered; every folk epic attests to this fact, from the Gilgamesh epic of the Sumerians and the Iliad of the Greeks to the Hebrew Bible in its first five books, and in many epics composed since those.

To attain to a position of eminence of any sort in any society means to have won out in a competition with rivals, who presumably wanted the same advantage and were beaten in the struggle for them. In an orderly society, the terms and conditions of the competition are agreed on in advance, but this does not rule out the frustration experienced by the losers, who are thereby committed to expressions of hatred, anger, and even rage. The entire history of the human species has been characterized by acts of violence resulting from the prevalence of hate. Can we believe that the besieged Trojans were not possessed by such emotions before the fall of Troy, or by the Canaanites before their conquest by the Israelites? Hate does not seem to have had its chroniclers because it has never been a popular feeling, but we may be sure that it has always existed.

How deeply hatred is imbedded in human nature and how easily it can be aroused is often exemplified by the behavior of the spectators of professional sports. In some athletic events, ice hockey for instance, players have been known to fight and even damage each other at the expense of the game from which they make a living and support families. In South America, men have died from the effects of excess enthusiasm when it leads to open physical conflict, and this over a soccer game whose intent is merely to entertain, another example of the phenomenon of love turning into hate. It is always there just below the surface, ready to take over and dictate relevant actions.

Hatred would not have survived for so long and been so prevalent if it offered no advantage; but of course it does. Survival to some extent depends upon it. Perhaps in its absence rivals would not be challenged or eliminated, but it is part of the equipment of defense, an emotion which might arouse an individual to danger and set him to protect himself.

How very good it would be if things had been arranged otherwise, if cooperation was always the rule and not merely the exception. Among other animals there is rivalry: for feeding grounds, for females, and often merely for the establishment of a feeling of superiority, which is no doubt connected with both needs. But in any case, self-defense begins with the sense of danger, and there is danger when there is a rival. The whole process of dealing with a rival, reaching out, so to speak, to take care of a threat before it can do damage, begins with hate, which in this connection is only the recognition that a danger exists.

Yet it remains true that hate is not only unproductive: despite its species advantage, it is destructive to the hater. Nothing good comes of anything but positive attitudes and actions, for hate is negative, and if it does not succeed in reaching the hated object, it does reach the hater himself and destroys him little by little because it poisons and thwarts all his other instincts and intentions. The evidence for this is the extent to which anyone in the grip of a powerful hate feels ill; he suffers from inaction where action is clearly called for. A religion whose adherents express their religious feelings by hating others loses its value as a religion. Once the full force of hate is allowed to go unchecked, purgation can come only from destruction, and that is not always possible; moreover, it may be followed by remorse even where it has been successful.

The burning question, in which the future of our species is involved, is: what is to be done about hate? No good answer has been suggested; meanwhile people go blithely on with the business of killing.

Many of the difficulties we encounter result from our efforts to live up to our false image of ourselves as benign, generally well-intentioned, and with no inclination at all to violence. For the ugly truth is that we are not as entirely given over to the expressions of good will as we like to think. We are, instead, ambivalent creatures, and in our quiet periods — which I freely admit are many — we tend to think of ourselves as ruled by love rather than hate, with an instinct for peace rather than war, and on the whole, well-meant with regard to our fellow man. I have tried to show that this is not the case, and I have tried to make as good an argument as I could against it.

Perhaps the start of the solution to our problem is to recognize that there is a problem, for no one ever resolved a difficulty who did not think that he had one. If we are truly like that, truly as much devoted to destruction as to construction, as ready to destroy as to build, truly, in other words, as ready to hate as to love, and eager, moreover, to act on our feelings either way, then our first solution is to recognize our own genuine nature, to admit to ourselves that it is not all good, and to be prepared to deal with it on those terms.

We dare not give up the capacity for aggression lest we cease to be human; we need to retain it, provided it can be channelled in useful ways. An ambitious and vigorous individual who plays by the rules in his efforts to impose himself on others may make a valuable contribution to the culture. We want him to be positive rather than negative, but how are we to make this distinction in his favor? In institutional terms, how do we get to foster agriculture and industry but not also wars? No way has yet been found to accomplish this difference; but the search must be continued, for it is our only hope.

CHAPTER XIII

ON MYSTERY

I

What is mystery exactly? The term has always baffled thinkers, some insisting that by its very nature its object cannot be defined nor even described. There is, of course, some merit to this claim, but I intend to examine the problem once again, and my justification is that I will be approaching it from the perspective of a fresh thesis. The thesis in question can be stated quite simply: it is that *mystery is indivisible*. The remainder of this paper will be devoted to a discussion of the implications of such a proposition, which are quite far-reaching.

All such investigations may well begin with an examination of the language involved; and in this particular case it is more urgent than usual, for the term 'mystery' is common enough, but there does not seem to be any general agreement about it. Offhand, it is employed to name something which in our experience has not been explained, either because it is inexplicable or for the reason that we have not approached it properly. If it is inexplicable, then we have gone in that direction as far as it is possible to go, but I see nothing to be gained by shutting off inquiry, since that would leave things exactly as they were; so I suggest instead another approach.

Obviously it is possible to say quickly that mystery concerns either some part of existence or the whole of existence. If it concerns only a part, then mystery is divisible and we are not conducting the promised investigation. Only if it concerns the whole can it be indivisible, so we may start there, even though that leaves much to be explained.

II

We are, however, moving ahead of our argument, and so I shall fall back upon the more sobering question of definition: what, exactly, is meant by 'mystery'?

Any examination should begin with a careful consideration of the term, and to this end I propose to look first at the various definitions given in the *Oxford English Dictionary*. There we find listed twelve distinctly different ones, which are divided into two sets, describing "theological" and "non-theological" uses, respectively.

The theological uses are : (1) in or by mystical presence; (2) a religious truth known only from divine revelation; (3) a religious ordinance or rite, e.g., the Eucharist; (4) an incident in the life of our Lord or the saints regarded as having a special significance.

The non-theological uses are : (5) a hidden or secret thing; a matter unexplained or inexplicable; beyond human knowledge or comprehension; a riddle or enigma; (6) the condition or property of being secret; (7) obscure or hidden; (8) an action or practice kept secret; (9) certain secret rites in the religious systems of Ancient Greece, Rome, Egypt; (10) the name of a miracle play; (11) a medicine man, his 'mysteries'; (12) technically, a fly for fishing; and an alloy of platinum, tin and copper imitating gold; a kind of plum cake.

These, then, are the various ways in which the word has been used recently, and the first thing to do will be to purge the definition of its prejudices and cultural narrowness, for our aim is not to defend a corner but to make a careful and disinterested inquiry so far as that is possible. That it was not possible for the editors of the *Oxford English Dictionary* is made evident by the distinction they drew between theological and non-theological uses of the term 'mystery'. They gave the example of Christianity as theological and of ancient religions which are presumably non-theological. This was so prejudiced and partisan that I had to consider it of no value for my purpose and so felt justified in passing on to other definitions.

After due reflection, I thought it best under the circumstances to confine my study to the fifth definition in which mystery is not supernatural or divine but rather "a hidden or secret thing; a matter unexplained or inexplicable; beyond human knowledge or comprehension; a riddle or enigma."

III

If there is anything in the world which persistently remains "unexplained", then we can expect it to be regarded — unjustifiably, perhaps — as "inexplicable." The case for the proposition that what has not been explained cannot be, is far from made, and so we do not know whether there is anything which is inherently a "hidden" or a "secret thing." What is it, precisely, that is found in this condition? We can safely venture a guess by widening out the inquiry by means of a further question: *why is there what there is?*

On various occasions various answers have been given, none of them, however, acceptable to everyone; and while it usually turns out that the false beliefs we entertain today will serve as the truths we live by tomorrow, obviously none has worked out to the satisfaction of the whole of humanity. Cultural escarpments are also those of 'world' religions, but the fact is that the human species, throughout its long history and with all of its superior intelligence, has never settled for once and all anything of importance to it. Of course, many of the best minds and spirits have occupied themselves with the problem, and it is fair to say that those who have called on the imagination as an aid to the understanding are, in a certain sense, contemporaries.

On examination, the question, *why is there what there is?* promises to be unexpectedly all-embracing. In the general sense of the deepest meaning, no answer has been made but an important step has been taken. The failure to find an answer, despite the number of searchers and the generations of inquirers, points to a positive conclusion of its own. Everything there is has the common property of remaining unexplained, with the conclusion that in this respect, even if only in this respect, there is a unity to the universe. All is one, taken as unexplained. But if everything is a mystery, then nothing is *especially* mysterious, for it is all a mystery together. Thus the failure of explanation leads through the unity of the universe to our original thesis that mystery is indivisible.

So run the dictates of reason, and reason tends to be destructive of traditional theologies. None is able to stand up to such an examination, and no organized religion has yet been devised to meet the challenge. The opposition is nothing new; it was recognized at least as early as Tertullian who advised accepting that which is absurd, and perhaps much earlier with Xenophanes who made the assertion, repeatedly and in many ways, that the concept of divinity was a construction of the human imagination.

But there is another approach altogether, and it is contained in the second group of definitions from the *Oxford Dictionary*. This one concerns the "riddle or enigma" caused by the fact that the explanation of mystery "lies beyond human knowledge or comprehension."

Those who adhere to this alternative contend that the way to approach mystery is through the feelings or emotions. All who recommend faith as the only proper avenue to the ultimate mystery are suggesting this solution. "Why is there what there is?" We have not arrived at the answer by searching through reason or fact; we can only come at it through the lofty feelings called emotions. Faith properly embraced is the emotion that results from the feeling that a proposition is true, but we forget that the proposition could be false and still give rise to the feeling.

The contention often receives support from those who otherwise regard themselves as rationalists, but it is the feeling itself that we are, properly speaking, concerned with here, not the proposition, and the feeling only in its most exalted form, expressed as an emotion. Worshippers in churches, synagogues, and mosques are not expected to think, only to feel, and what they are asked to feel is the presence of divinity: something called out in them by ceremony, music, and ritual, which they are expected to believe has a special divine origin, even though what "lies beyond human knowledge or comprehension" is not necessarily validated by feeling.

Yet if they would not believe, they would still live, and their lives are guided, their customs and institutions established, by separate and distinctly different versions of the one ultimate mystery. Although it remains indivisible, they conduct their lives in terms of its divisions and employ their faith to oppose those having a different faith whose segments of the mystery are not the same as their own; they live, in other words, by proximate answers to unanswerable questions, for they cannot bear to think that mystery is indivisible.

It has been noted that there are no false feelings; the feelings we have we *do* have. The error lies in supposing that such feelings validate anything external. The feelings can be centrally aroused or externally stimulated and only tell us about ourselves; but they are internal in any case and do not necessarily reveal anything about the external world. There is no way to check on what we read from the feelings, and especially when we credit them with reporting about entities and processes which allegedly lie beyond nature. There are so many all-embracing faiths, and they are all so comforting, that we cannot afford to take seriously their claims concerning the divine. The feelings, in short, cannot legitimately be expected to answer the question *why there is what there is?*

IV

If, indeed, after all these millennia we have failed to discover an answer, perhaps it is time to try a new approach. For now the question we have been investigating suggests still another: *what is there?*

The chief result of every important new discovery is the general area of ignorance it opens to inquiry. The successful solving of one problem gives rise to a host of others which are often more complex and extensive, and whose solution, if it is to be reached at all, will necessarily involve the work of many investigators. Progress in knowledge, in other words, is made at the cost of uncovering new puzzlements, so that any final understanding of what there is must be indefinitely postponed.

The longer the investigation of the material universe continues, the more the mystery deepens, for that universe is both more intensive and more extensive than had been supposed.

Its intensive nature has been made evident by the studies of particle physics, where every major advance discloses the existence of smaller and smaller constituents. What began as an investigation of the properties of the atom has now disclosed that there are many such, and so atoms are now believed to be made up of particles smaller still: not only electrons, protons, and the like, but also their quark constituents. It is even suspected that there are still smaller elements composing the quarks.

At the other end of the investigation, the material universe proves to be vastly extensive. The galaxies, of which solar systems are tiny parts, stretch many light-years across, and there are millions of them. Suns have been found which are thousands of times larger and brighter than ours, and there are queer objects we don't begin to understand.

We ourselves, together with our immediate environment, evidently have only a relative importance, shrinking with every gain in knowledge made in particle physics and astronomy, while the new ignorances both areas entail invite us to wonder.

Can it be, then, that mystery consists only in what lies *outside* knowledge as a recognition of the fact that there is more that we don't understand than that we do? The evidence is now clear that there is a grey area between the two, and that we have reserved the term 'mystery' for only the unknown when perhaps it should be shifted to include the known, which is mysterious enough. The mystics have in the past found their subject matter in a blade of grass or a visible star; but we ought to be able to do better than that because now we can fix it at more elaborate levels.

The new idea in the world is the mystery of the known. We still live our emotional life with familiar objects, that is to say, with the knowledge we inherited from previous generations. But now there is fresh knowledge and an overwhelming amount of it, more acquired in the last century than in all the previous ones, and our emotions have not yet caught up with it. It may have to be consolidated before it can have an impact, but inevitably, it must change our sense of mystery.

What this will all mean it is impossible to predict, chiefly because feelings are indescribable; but it most certainly will come to us, and that is inevitable, if not soon, when the accumulation of knowledge has slowed sufficiently to make consolidation possible. Emotions can be responsive to wholes as well as parts, but the knowledge of the universe cannot reasonably be organized until there is some decrease in its rapid acceleration. When we are in a position to add up what we have learned, we will be better able to determine how we feel about it; and when that happens, mystery will have been given a new meaning.

V

Meanwhile, of course, we are obliged to deal with systems of belief as we have inherited them, and we have inherited them collected under the rubric of theologies. Now, theologies are undertakings by organized religions to defend faith by means of reason. Each pretends to an unacknowledged exclusivity which rejects the validity of all the others. Thus each makes the assumption that mystery is divisible, with the further assumption that one division is alone justifiable.

I know of the existence of only two movements in the other direction, movements intended to unify rather than divide. One is the religion of the Baha'i, the other the philosophical conception of the unlimited community.

The Baha'i movement, an offshoot of Islam, began in the middle of the nineteenth century and very soon went its own way, regarding every 'universal' religion as the equal of every other in their mutual claims to the unity of mankind. Everyone enters into the Baha'i through his own organized religion as a means, with the center as an end. The Baha'i faith, which includes Abraham, Moses, Jesus, and Mohammed among its prophets, emphasizes world unity and treats religious truth as a relative and evolving concept.

There is an inherent contradiction in its doctrine, which claims that the way to enter the Baha'i is through some exclusive faith, as though the sum of exclusive faiths would equal a non-exclusive one. But to accept Judaism, Christianity, or Islam is to deny the others, at least by implication, and that is a rather inadequate way to attain to a universalist faith.

The Baha'i has failed as a world movement; and even though it has some members in Iran and the United States, the total is not very impressive. But it *can* claim that according to its tenets, mystery is indivisible. Small comfort that appears to be. In Iran at the present moment, members of the Baha'i are being executed wholesale by Moslem extremists on orders from their leader, the Ayatollah Khomeini, and may soon disappear there along with others the government feels as a threat to its tenuous hold on power.[1]

Turning now to the other movement intended to unify rather than divide the conception of an "unlimited community," there is the foundation of the ethics of Charles S. Peirce. He had a unique program, for he sought to found the indivisibility of mystery on a rational argument whose approach lay through the use of logic and fact, the essence of which consists in the undeniable statement that a sufficient number of finite existences adds up to an infinite existence. Nothing lasts forever except the succession of failures. He saw that while every discrete thing, including individual man, all societies, and even civilizations, must eventually perish, they do not "collectively fail" because they are parts of an unbroken order of brief-lived things.

Thus while every finite thing ends eventually, all succeed in contributing to an unlimited community of existing things which extend beyond all bounds, and we are led to put our faith not in any particular absolute but in the probability of infinite unity. Peirce followed his argument to its logical conclusion. He said,

It seems to me that we are driven to this, that logicality inevitably requires that our interests shall *not* be limited. They must not stop at our own fate but must embrace the whole community. This community again, must not be limited, but must extend to all races of beings.... It must reach, however vaguely, beyond this geological epoch, beyond all bounds. But all this requires a conceived identification of one's interest with those of an unlimited community.[2]

Both the Baha'i's and Peirce's unlimited communities have failed as world movements, as indeed they must have done, for to succeed, every human being would have had to become converted.

There are also other considerations. We must remember that even if we were to admit the truth of the thesis that mystery is indivisible, the indivisibility applies only to the mystery. Mystery by its very nature is already split off from all else that is not mystery; and since mystery is something special, the rest of existence, which is by far the preponderance of it, must overwhelm it in the end. There is ordinary life to be managed in its endless detail: a living to be earned, children raised, all of the petty details and exhausting efforts working in the same direction: away from the attempts at ultimate explanation. That is left to specialists of all sorts, but chiefly to religious leaders. The devisive movements of religions take precedence, at least in their importunity, over those that tend to unite. The unity of mankind is defeated by politicians, by special interest groups, even by rival claimants to the right to speak for the unity of mankind, and it is defeated still more by those whose interests and activities are inherently criminal: by murderers, robbers, and rapists, by revolutionaries and terrorists, by all those, in fact, whose actions tend to divide rather than unite.

In a word, men seem to be hopelessly divided by circumstance yet united in a common quest, for the sense of mystery is also one which will never be completely satisfied. The road to a comprehensive universal belief begins with universal doubt but does not end there. It can end only with what beliefs mankind succeeds in holding in common. Until they can overcome all the limited positive beliefs that divide them, they will never be able to take the important step of recognizing that mystery is indivisible.

VI

I began this investigation by asking, what is mystery and what can be done to resolve it? I have answered the first question by arguing that mystery is indivisible and therefore, since it concerns nothing less than the whole of being, remains unexplained; for a quality can only be accepted, it cannot be resolved. As to what can be done about it, I think there is a practical answer, and that is the religious enterprise, but immediately a caveat must be entered against all of the usual religious procedures because they are devisive. We must remember the salient fact that the whole of mankind comprises no more than a single interbreeding species.

Now if it is true that mystery is indivisible, and further, that mankind is a single species, then there can be one only one religious enterprise: *to emphasize the similarities that exist between all peoples and to minimize their differences.* There can be nothing else in human life so important. It is not a new idea, for occasionally it has been suggested in one form or another; the great religious founders have implied it where they have not said it directly. Buddha, Confucius, Moses, Jesus, Mohammed, all have suggested something closely resembling such an insight.

What has followed them in each case, however, has been the result of another force in human life that cuts across it, one that has a more immediate demand to make, the need for food. For millions of early years, the pre-human species and finally, also the human, lived as nomads on the herds they followed, in a hunting culture which made killing a primary contribution to survival. Before man can concern himself with his ultimate fate, he must get rid of the pangs of hunger.

When not too many thousands of years ago, agriculture and animal husbandry changed his way of life, it did not reduce killing, only eliminated hunting and ever since then, the animals have been penned up and available whenever there is a need to kill them for food.

That took care of hunger, but it did not take care of aggression. It only frustrated it; the hunting instinct was still there, so that an unholy alliance had to be struck between the need to kill and religion. Militant religious movements were the result, and they have, for the most part, dominated religious activities despite the fact that they are inherently contradictory.

Thus the religious movement which recognizes that human similarities be emphasized and human differences minimized has found few followers and little practice. From the medieval crusades and the Templars to the pitched battles fought by rival Buddhist monasteries in early Japan, the very antithesis of the religious impulse has prevailed. We find it operating still today in the armed conflict between Protestant and Catholic Christians in northern Ireland.

What is at issue is a pair of conflicting demands, both of which are fundamental: the demand for immediate survival, represented by the need for food, and the demand for ultimate survival, represented by the need for identification with the universe or its cause. More often than not, the two demands are joined in the single organization of a militant church which either calls for violent action or, at the very least, condones it, so that the social and cultural effort to dominate material resources takes on the character of an unholy alliance in favor of the creator. Those who, in the name of a church, engage in devisive action may be serving an individual need to survive, but they are doing so at the expense of the religious impulse and so also at the expense of damage to a common humanity.

CHAPTER XIV

THE GLOBAL JEWISH CONTRIBUTION

I

It has been noted by many observers, both Jewish and non-Jewish, that the contribution of the Jews to human culture has been unusually large in proportion to their numbers. Throughout the centuries, the Jews have produced more than their share of religion, philosophy, art, and science. How have they managed to do it?

There have been many attempts to explain this phenomenon, and some have merit. The practical advantages of a successful explanation would be enormous, for it would give us what, at present, we do not have: the technique for developing original contributors to culture, for turning out producers. Here, then, is one more guess at the riddle.

Today most zoologists insist that the entire human population consists in a single gene pool and constitutes a single species, since any two members of it can produce fertile offspring. The racial account of the Jews is therefore false. Perhaps there is a clue in the ability of the Jews to maintain their identity as a social group for four millennia under all sorts of adverse conditions. This fact in itself is not an explanation, however, and we shall have to look farther afield. Many specialists have made suggestions but have reached no agreement. Here, then, is one more theory which I put forward for examination and criticism, one based on the biological theory of evolution, including its more recent versions, and on anthropology.

II

Let me begin by calling attention to a fact which has been known to the biologists since Darwin. The isolation of breeding groups has a favorable effect on the evolution of the species. Habitat often provides the occasion for such isolation, as Darwin observed in the Galapagos Islands. The isolation referred to here is reproductive as well as spatial. If interbreeding is possible through an entire species, then fitness becomes so broad and must become adjusted to so many various conditions that development is arrested. But when a particular region is separated spatially, the breeding group within it is better able to adjust to local conditions and so to develop differences from the remainder of the species. Thus evolutionary change is promoted by the existence of conditions providing the requisite isolation.

The ideal situation, according to Sewall Wright, is a large population effectively divided into a number of small partially isolated breeding populations. The optimum conditions for populations exclude complete isolation. Populations which have such isolation tend toward extinction. The favorable kind of isolation is only partial. Wright has shown that if there are relatively small numbers in each particular breeding population, the probabilities of combinations will exceed expectations, and as a consequence, there will be an increase in variety and novelty.

III

What is true in respect to the breeding populations of sub-human animal species may be equally true of the human species. The optimum conditions for human communities include partial isolation but exclude complete isolation. Communities which are completely isolated tend to disappear. The favorable kind of isolation is partial, and indeed partial isolation seems to be essential.

Now let us introduce an element which exists among all animals but plays an inordinately large role among humans, the element of material culture. The outstanding factor in the recent career of the species *Homo sapiens* is the immense role played in his environment by his material culture. By material culture will be meant those elements of the material environment which have been altered through human agency into languages and tools. Human societies transmit externally the knowledge and the skills to utilize material culture by means of learning, a process which has been described as epigenetic inheritance. It is not often recognized that such epigenetic inheritance functions as an isolating mechanism. The culture of every society differs from that of every other. People distrust and even fear anything which is different. They always use their own customs and institutions, their own material culture, as the standard of what is normal.

Now because there is such a phenomenon as cultural mobility, the contacts between cultures are inevitable. When the cultures are more or less equal, one or both tends to be destroyed in a war. When they are unequal, the majority tends to absorb the minority, perhaps with some adaptive change on the part of the majority. When a minority culture is weak, it tends to merge with the culture of the majority and to disappear. But when it is strong, it offers a barrier to cultural extinction and is able to maintain itself throughout the interchange. It is a well-known fact that cultural encounters and interactions tend to be very productive on both sides. Cultural origination, as well as cultural diffusion, may result from the contacts between cultures if they are sufficiently dissimilar to provide mutual challenges and stimulations. The kind of partial isolation which is favorable could arise from such a situation as the contact between a majority culture and a minority culture. "Majority" and "minority" are intended here to have merely numerical reference. Partial isolation would then mean, from the point of view of the majority culture, division into an externally inherited material culture on the one hand, and cultural pressures from an environing alien culture on the other.

At this point, another peculiarly human factor enters the picture: the very slow process of maturation. The segmentation of the species into isolated breeding populations furnishes the specialization, while the slowness of maturation permits the young to absorb it thoroughly as a matter of epigenetic inheritance. In other words, the external cultural inheritance of the isolated community has time to make itself felt because of the length of the learning period in the human individual.

IV

In the light of the biological data set forth above, let us look at the history of the Jewish people. Since the conquest of Jerusalem in 597 B.C. and its destruction by the Babylonians fourteen years later, the Jews have been scattered, but they learned how to support Judaism when permanently away from their homeland. The dispersion took place under the Persian Empire, but curiously the connections with Jerusalem were continued and even encouraged by the Persians. In the Diaspora, Judaism had a plurality of centers rather than a single one. It was wherever there were Jews.

The Jewish people have never actively engaged in missionary work, but since the Persian period they have kept the doors open to proselytes. Thus wherever they happened to be, the interaction with the neighboring societies was not prohibited by any practice of exclusiveness. There is much evidence of prolonged interaction. Maimonides wrote his medical books in Arabic, and an enormous literature exists in Yiddish, which is a combination of archaic Rhineland German with Hebrew, with some later Slavic admixtures.

One outstanding fact stares us in the face, and this is the combination of the Diaspora with the supreme effort to maintain a cultural integrity within an isolated breeding group. The Jews are, and always have been, few in number, and in terms of breeding groups, this has been part of their strength. Everywhere they go they constitute a minority because as a group they maintain a cultural autonomy. It is true, of course, that the group usually becomes somewhat eroded at the edges. Some converts are made to other religions, and some members of other religions become converted to Judaism. But on the whole and at the center, the integrity of the traditional group is jealously guarded.

This is, of course, not only their strength but also the source of their cultural contribution. For wherever the Jews establish themselves among other cultures as a minority, they interact locally with the prevailing culture; they are affected by it, and they make their own peculiar cultural contribution to it. The amount of such a contribution will often(though not always) be at a higher rate than that of the majority. Thus for the Jews as a whole, the rate of production of material culture is extraordinarily impressive. The Jewish contribution to religion, philosophy, the arts, and the sciences is higher than that of a proportionate population.

The pressures of the culture of an alien population constitute an important challenge to the locally isolated Jewish community. What we are always dealing with is a combination of the Jewish cultural inheritance with the culture of the local majority population. Some contributions have proved happier than others. The combination of the Jewish with the Greek culture produced the Neo-Platonism of Philo which, through the medium of Plotinus, permeated the theologies of Islam and Christianity. The combination of the Jewish with the Roman culture produced Christianity itself. The combination of the Jewish with the German culture produced an extraordinarily high number of originative intellectuals: among the artists, Heine and Mendelssohn; among the scientist, Marx, Wassermann, Freud, Einstein, and Meitner; and among the philosophers, Husserl and Cassirer.

There would be a very genuine danger to human evolution in the concept of one world if this were to mean a single culture for all peoples. The tendency toward "cultural homogenization," as Muller calls it, is not desirable. Should the species become genetically uniform and culturally similar, so that there would be no isolated breeding populations and all social groups everywhere would have to cope with the same set of conditions, the evolution of the species would be definitely threatened. The security of humanity is thus seen to depend upon the tolerance of difference. Some moral code is an ingredient of every culture, and morality, for the most part, is never more than culture-wide. Morality, in other words, is culturally conditioned. Every nation has its own culture, even though there is an overlap to some extent. But such overlap must not only be the same for all, but it must be of a special kind. There must be a common denominator among the moralities of all cultural groups, and it must include the principle that the existence of a difference in moralities is not only tenable, but necessary.

Such a principle the Jewish dispersion happily has provided. The Jews exist in far flung, partially isolated, breeding populations, both influencing and being influenced by the local majority populations. The widespread distribution is impressive, and includes the dark-skinned Falashas of Abyssinia; the Turkish Jews of Salonica in the fifteenth century; the Jewish community in Kai feng Fu in China, rediscovered by missionaries in 1607 and probably a branch of the Persian Jews; the Jews of Cochin, India, divided into three castes according to color and speaking both Hebrew and Malayalam, the Dravidian dialect of their Hindu neighbors; to say nothing of the large Jewish communities scattered throughout Europe and the Americas. The device of a single society with its culture which is both mobile and worldwide, and consists of a great number of partially isolated breeding populations, each of which maintains available for exchange a cultural autonomy, is, from the point of view of humanity as a whole, extremely valuable, and it is exclusively Jewish.

One measure of culture is the richness of differences, one measure of the advancement of culture is the extent to which differences in culture are able to interact. For it is with cultures, as with genetics, that progress relies upon a process of fertilization, and this process has a superior product chiefly when in biology, the two sexes, and in culture, the two civilizations, are markedly different so that each brings to the mixture elements which the other could not. Cultural mobility has been at its highest in the case of the Jews who have therefore been able to provide the mixing partner to cultures throughout the world.

NOTES

CHAPTER V

1. *Nature*, 275, 478 (1978).
2. *Nature*, 252, 216 (1974).

CHAPTER VIII

1. *On the Orator*, 3.35.141.
2. *Phaedrus*, 279.
3. *Panegyricus*, 50.
4. *The Attic Nights of Aulus Gellius J.C. Rolfe, trans.* (London 1946, William Heinemann). vol. I, pp. 277-278.
5. *Sophist*, 231A.
6. *Theaetetus*, 232.
7. *Gorgias*, 457E.
8. The advent of the culture of Hellenism marked an abrupt change. Twice in the two previous centuries, the Roman senate had decreed the banishment of all philosophers and rhetoricians, first in 161 B.C. and again in A.D. 89 in the reign of Domitian. Cf. *Attic Nights of Aulus Gellius*, Vol. III, Book XV, chapter XI.
9. *Lives*, 481.
10. Cf. Albin Lesky, *A History of Greek Literature* (New York 1963, Crowell), pp. 829-845. Also H. I. Marrou, *A History of Education in Antiquity*, G. Lamb, trans. (New York 1977, Sheed & Ward), pp. 201 and 210 ff.
11. A typical example: when the sophist Hadrian performed his duties as occupant of the chair of rhetoric at Athens, he wore very expensive clothes, bedecked himself with precious gems, and used to go down to his lectures in a carriage with silver-mounted bridles; and always after the lecture he would go home envied by all, escorted by those who loved Hellenic culture, from all parts of the world. Philostratus, *Lives*, 587.
    That was not all:
    The Emperor (Marcus) admired him greatly, and exalted him to the skies by grants and gifts. By grants, I mean the right to dine at the expense of the state, a seat of honour at the public games, immunity from taxes, priestly offices ... and by gifts I mean gold and silver, horses, slaves .... *Ibid.*, 589.
12. For an apt analogy, see the fashion of pursuing rhetoric as practiced in Tudor England, e.g., Warren Taylor, *Tudor Figures of Rhetoric* (Chicago 1937, University of Chicago Libraries). Dr. Taylor's Preface is illuminating.

CHAPTER IX

1. J. Dollard, L.W. Doob, O.H. Mowrer, and R.R. Sears, *Frustration and Aggression* (New Haven, Conn. 1939, Yale University Press.
2. *Ibid.*, p. 11
3. Arnold H. Buss, *The Psychology of Aggression* (New York 1961, Wiley), p. 1.
4. Konrad Lorentz, *Das Sogennante Bose* (Vienna 1963, Dr. G. Borotha-Schoeler).

5. J.D. Carthy and P.J. Ebling (eds.), *The Natural History of Aggression* (London 1965, Academic Press).
6. George A. Miller, Eugene Galanter and Karl H. Pribram, *Plans and The Structure of Behavior* (New York 1960, Holt, Rinehart & Winston), p. 16.
7. Sir Julian Huxley, *Perspect. Biol. Med.*, 61155, (1963).

CHAPTER X

1. Vincent Descombes, *Modern French Philosophy* (Cambridge 1980, University Press), pp. 13-14.
2. Ibid., p. 13.
3. Irving M. Copi, *Symbolic Logic*, third ed. (New York 1970, Macmillan), p. 189.
4. Jon Barwise, ed., *Handbook of Mathematical Logic*, article by C. Smorynski (Amsterdam 1977, North-Holland), p. 844.
5. *Op. cit., loc. cit.*

CHAPTER XI

1. Nicholas Rescher, *Hypothetical Reasoning* (Amsterdam 1964, North-Holland Publishing Co.), p. 47.
2. *Collected Papers of Charles Sanders Peirce* (Cambridge, Mass. 1931-35, Harvard University Press), 6.493, 6.458, 6.613.

CHAPTER XII

1. James K. Feibleman, *The Quiet Rebellion* (New York 1972, Horizon Press), chapter 13.
2. Irenaus Eibl-Eibesfeldt, *Love and Hate*, G. Strachan, trans. (London 1971, Methuen), especially chapter 5.
3. James K. Feibleman "Technology and Human Nature," in *The Southwestern Journal of Philosophy*, x, 35-41, (1979).
4. James K. Feibleman *Mankind Behaving: Human Needs and Material Culture*, (Charles C. Thomas 1963, Springfield, Ill.)
5. *Albert Camus, Reistance, Rebellion and Death*, J. O'brien trans. (New York 1961, Knopf), p. 18.
6. *Opocit.*

CHAPTER XIII

1. *The New York Times*, October 18, 1981, p. 10.
2. C.S. Peirce, *Collected Papers* (Cambridge 1932, Harvard University Press), 2.654. For other references and a more extended discussion see James K. Feibleman, *An Introduction to The Philosophy of Charles S. Peirce* (Cambridge 1969, the MIT Press), pp. 382-386.

Bibliography

Theodosius, Dobzhansky, *Mankind Evolving* (New Haven 1962, Yale University Press).

Louis (ed.), Finkelstein, *The Jews: Their History, Culture and Religion*. 2 Vols. (New York 1949, Harpwr & Bros.)

Garrett, Hardin, *Nature and Man's Fate*. (New York 1961, New American Library).

Ernest, Mayr, *Animal Species and Evolution*. (Cambridge, Mass., The Belknap Press of Harvard University Press).

Hermann J., Muller, "The prospect of genetic progress," in Boyko, Hug (ed.) *Science and the Future of Mankind*. (The Hague 1961, Uitgevery Dr. W. Junk). p. 71.

C.H., Waddington, *The Ethical Animal*. (London 1960, Allen & Unwin).

Sewall., Wright, "Evolution in Mendelian populations", *Genetics*, Vol. 16 (1931), pp. 97-159.

"The 'age and area' concept extended", *Ecology*, Vol. 22 (1941), pp. 345-47.

INDEX